NATIONAL PRAISE FOR
DEREK FOSTER

"His (Derek Foster's) seductively simple approach...
resonated with tens of thousands of Canadians who
bought his bestselling books..."   — *Globe and Mail*

"Thanks to a healthy stock portfolio, Derek Foster
retired when he was 34 years old."   — *Toronto Star*

"Thanks to a solid investment plan and a knack for
picking the right stocks he (Derek Foster) was able to
retire, mortgage-free, at the age of 34."

— *ROBTV (forerunner to BNN)*

"He's (Derek Foster) playing his very own game,
which he's winning..."   — *National Post*

"...— and he did it by turning the whole concept of
what it means to save for retirement on its head."

— *Moneysense Magazine*

"While Warren Buffett is known as the Oracle of
Omaha, investment whiz Derek Foster could be
labelled the Wise Man of Wasaga Beach."

— *Toronto Sun*

The Worried Boomer

No Pension?

Not Wealthy?

Here's YOUR Plan!

The Idiot-Proof Retirement
Strategy from

The Idiot Millionaire

Derek Foster

FOSTER, UNDERHILL FINANCIAL PRESS

Library and Archives Canada Cataloguing in Publication

Foster, Derek, 1970–

 The worried boomer : no pension? not wealthy? here's your plan! / Derek Foster.

ISBN 978-0-9736960-5-9

 1. Retirement income—Planning. 2. Investments.
 3. Finance, Personal.

I. Title.
HG179.F678 2011 332.024'0140971 C2011-907231-9

Published by
Foster, Underhill Financial Press
900 Greenbank Road, Suite 508
Ottawa, ON K2J 4P6
Canada
Phone toll free at: 1 888 686 STOP (1 888 686 7867)
or 613 823 2143
www.stopworking.ca

Design/formatting/production: WeMakeBooks.ca
Printed and bound in Canada

LEGAL DISCLAIMER

—

This book is intended to show you a strategy that you might want to consider for investing.

However, you must realize that I am not a professional with regard to any of the information I've provided in this book. I am merely presenting a strategy that I feel might be of interest to you. I am not an expert in economic, legal, taxation, investing, realty, or any other financial or related matters. The examples I provide are just that—examples. These are intended for illustrative purposes only. They are not an indication of what rate of return or future amount of money you might have if you followed the specific examples. They are only presented to illustrate the general concepts. Before initiating any of the strategies outlined, seek the advice of a competent professional to help you.

The book is intended as a general guide and should not be viewed as the ultimate source for financial information. Further research is needed and assistance must be sought from a qualified expert, before any action is taken by the reader. For further information, there is a recommended reading list at the back of this book. The information in these books might be incomplete, inaccurate, or out of date, so the reader should verify any of this information before acting on it.

For full disclosure, I must say that I (Derek Foster) may own some of the securities mentioned in this book. The reader must also understand that any investing activity entails certain degrees of risk. Although lists of securities are presented in the book, the reader must understand that these securities do carry risk and should seek the advice from a qualified expert before acting upon any of the information.

Furthermore, this book might contain various errors, omissions, or mistakes of either a typographical nature or within the content itself. The reader must not rely on the accuracy of any of the information given, but should seek proper verification.

The author (Derek Foster) and the publisher (Foster Underhill Financial Press) shall have neither liability nor responsibility to any person or other legal entity with respect to any sort of loss or damage or perceived damage caused, or alleged to have been caused by the information provided in this book. By reading this, you fully accept these conditions. If for any reason, you do not with to be bound by any or all of the above conditions, you many simply return this book to the publisher for a full refund.

Acknowledgements

Once again, there are some individuals I would like to thank. My deepest gratitude goes to my wife, Hyeeun, who offered her patience and support during the writing of this book.

To my Mom, Tina Colonnese, a special thank you for your input and guidance. Your involvement was invaluable.

A special thank you goes out to Brian Weatherdon of Sovereign Wealth Management, who offered his expertise and knowledge whenever asked.

In addition, I appreciated the input from Glenn Hall and George von Jagow from TD Waterhouse, who offered their insights and experience.

To Grant Fowlie of Edward Jones, thank you for taking the time to offer your insights.

And finally to Donna Eon of the SPP for taking time to enlighten me on the ins and outs of their plan.

Thank you all!

TABLE OF CONTENTS

Your Financial Toolbox...
Which Tools Do YOU Need?   *65*

A Pension Plan For YOU –
Even if Your Employer
Doesn't Offer One!   *101*

Your Basic Retirement Checklist   *119*

How Much Would You
Pay for a Good Night's Sleep?   *127*

Giving Gifts – Do it Right!   *135*

PART III: ACTION   *143*

Retirement Action Workbook   *145*

"The longer you wait for the future, the shorter it will be."

Loesje (international free speech organization)

GETTING FULL USE
FROM THIS BOOK...

———

*"You cannot open a book without
learning something."*
Confucius

This book is divided into two parts. The first section is the main part, which will explain the various financial tools that are available to you in
your retirement planning arsenal (some of which
are relatively unknown to many people). The second part is the retirement action workbook. Here
you can calculate your own estimated retirement
income line-by-line in order to get an idea of
where you need to go financially.

One question you might ask yourself is,
"Should you consider a financial advisor"? That
decision will depend on you.

A friend of mine is mechanically inclined and he has mentioned to me on a number of occasions that it would be cheaper for me to change my own motor oil as opposed to having a garage do it. The garage charges $40-$50 per oil change and I could do it myself for approximately $20-$25. Although I am frugal, I know my limitations, and working on my vehicle is one of them. To me, it is not worth the effort to change my van's oil for the sake of a few dollars. To my friend, it's a no-brainer...he always changes his own oil.

The same scenario holds true for investing. I enjoy investing and have been doing it myself for years. You may also feel this same way and wish to create your own retirement action plan. If this is you, read this book and familiarize yourself with all the ideas and retirement tools. Once you've done that, complete the retirement action workbook and set your course for a carefree retirement. Fully knowing this detailed information will show you where you need to go and remove any doubts you might have about retiring.

However, I understand that not everyone is ready to take the retirement planning journey alone. If this is you, then read this book and understand all your investment options and THEN discuss these ideas with your advisor. This is the same approach you might take if your doctor told you that you had some sort of serious illness. If this happened, you would proactively learn all about your problem and look at the various options that would be available to you. Only AFTER doing this would you discuss your thoughts with your doctor and then seek his input. Knowledge is power!

Whatever path you decide, the ideas discussed in this book will help you reach a comfortable, worry-free retirement even if you are not wealthy and currently don't have a pension plan. It's time to solidify your financial future...

Are You Afraid of the Dark?

"FEAR: False Evidence
Appearing Real."
Unknown

When I was a kid, I was afraid of the dark. My mom, who has always had problems sleeping, had to create an environment that was "just right" in order to sleep. This meant sleeping in a dark, pitch black room. She wanted to make sure that I too would have good sleep and put solid, dark blinds up in my room. These blinds blocked any light from entering. Once the lights had been turned off, the room was very dark and I couldn't see anything. In my mind, there was not a specific monster or anything that I feared – it was just that once the lights were out

I did not know what was in my room – it was the fear of the UNKNOWN. If I got too scared, I would turn the light beside my bed back on and look around to get a clearer picture of who or what was in my room (and of course there were never any monsters – but sometimes the strange noises I heard were from our cat moving around the room). Once the light was on, the fear of the unknown disappeared.

Fear is a tool that has been used for centuries to motivate people to do things the ruling class wanted them to do. Propaganda machines work overtime during wartime to scare the populace into submission. If there is no war, one can be "manufactured". For example, North Koreans are constantly bombarded with announcements that the US is about to attack at any time! In medieval times, the fear of witchcraft led to the irrational punishment of many people who were burned alive at the stake.

Have you ever noticed how much marketing is based on fear or pointing out our flaws? Perhaps you need to be thinner. Magazine articles and TV shows will offer unrealistic body images and then companies will offer to sell you products which will allow you to reach that unattainable ideal; but only after you spend a lot of money on their products. Perhaps you need to become more fit or your kids need to be smarter...or more athletic. You need hair removal products...or hair replacement products. The companies that market these products would not spend millions of dollars on fear marketing if it did not work...and it does! By creating a sense of fear or self-doubt, these companies can motivate people to buy their products.

What about the fear of retiring without enough money? Have you ever thought,"I have not saved enough for retirement" or "How will I ever retire?" Perhaps these fears are reasonable – and perhaps not. Maybe you've been bombarded with information long enough that you feel if you are not saving every last penny you earn, your dinner during retirement will be cat food, which of course you will be eating from your new home – a cardboard box at the side of the road! These thoughts are the seeds of doubt that have been planted in your mind, creating a fear so that you feel compelled to do something. What should you do to avoid this dire fate? Well, you can avoid this terrible outcome if you...

Max out your RRSPs! Buy high-fee mutual funds! Seek the advice from a certain firm which will navigate the stormy seas for you and ensure you end up wealthy! If you act upon any of these strategies, you receive the proverbial "carrot". If you buy these products, you will live happily ever after. If you don't, the brutal "stick" of reality is ready to hit you!

I receive emails from people lamenting the fact that with increasing life expectancies they might run out of money in retirement. Another reader emailed me stating that both his parents and grandparents didn't have to confront the issue of lack of retirement money as life expectancy in previous generations was much less than today. Rather than rejoicing about the fact that people are living longer, healthier, more productive lives, many people have been scared silly about their financial future.

I want to alleviate that worry. It would be unrealistic for me to promise that once you've read this book you will experience sunshine and eternal bliss – but that is not what I'm promising. With this book, I want to "reach over" and "turn on the light" so that you can see things more clearly. I want to empower you by providing some answers to the unknown and pointing you in the right direction. With this book as your guide, you can take the necessary steps to create a reasonable retirement for yourself.

Once the unknown is gone, the worry and fear should also leave the room.

I don't know all the answers...but I did manage to retire in my 30s and become a millionaire through proper investing despite never having a regular high-paying career. I am not in the business of selling you investment products – so I am free to offer you unbiased ideas without favouring certain options over others.

You will notice throughout the book, I have referred to some of my previous books – but most often I will refer you to my fourth book, *STOP WORKING TOO: You Still Can!* This book highlighted many conservative investing strategies that might be suitable for you but to reiterate all the details would be a waste of your time. By using this book and referring to the others when necessary, you should be able to get a clearer picture of your situation and from that information, create your retirement action plan.

This book will show you how to take a holistic view of your situation. We will consider income sources you can already expect to receive once you retire – but you might not have been fully aware of them. We'll look at how your expenses might fall in retirement using my own real-life knowledge as a reference point.

We'll gather the pieces so that you won't have to take a huge leap of faith towards retirement – just a much smaller step in that direction. This book will provide you with some income-generating investment ideas that can allow you to take that step...providing you with the stable, lasting income you will need to retire.

Together, it's as simple as, "Lights, Camera, Action!

PART I

—

LIGHTS!

NORMAL PROBLEMS, NOVEL SOLUTIONS!

—

"A moment's insight is sometimes worth a life's experience."
Oliver Wendell Holmes

When I was a kid, there were a few different fictional books that I really enjoyed. In one series, a character nicknamed "Encyclopaedia Brown" solved a variety of cases using simple solutions. Another character known as "The Great Brain" used his intelligence to create a variety of entertaining situations. From these fictional tales I appreciated the potential benefits of "thinking outside the box."

In grade six I had to write a report on a famous person. I chose Henry Ford and was impressed with many of his accomplishments. His vision was to create an affordable vehicle for everyone and he accomplished this by creating efficient assembly lines. He continued to increase efficiency so that his "Model T" which cost $825 to purchase in 1908 fell to $290 by the 1920s. He ended up selling over 15 million of these cars – a phenomenal feat when you consider that this was almost 100 years ago!

While studying at university one of my business professors told a story about how the Ford assembly line was the model of efficiency for that era. One day, some businessmen were touring the Ford factory where they noticed that there was a lone employee to the side of the factory floor just sitting silently on a stool. They proceeded with their tour where they saw many men working away at assembling cars but when they finished their tour they noticed that one lone employee still sitting quietly on the stool. They asked Henry Ford why he had a worker who was just sitting there rather than working. Ford replied that, "he was thinking and that was his job." He went on to explain how this fellow had noticed that one simple improvement could be made to production which would save Ford a dollar or two per car. This idea saved

Ford millions of dollars over time. After that, he was promoted and his job was merely to come into the plant and think – which he did. Ford figured that if the fellow could come up with even one good idea a year, it would be well worth the money.

This idea of hiring someone to just "sit there and think" caught my attention. Today I am still intrigued by simple yet thoughtful solutions to problems. I enjoy hearing about "out of the box" solutions.

One of my favourite examples of this is the situation faced by NASA astronauts when they realized that regular ball point pens needed gravity to function properly. Since they operated in a zero-gravity environment in outer space, their pens would not work. Their solution was to spend millions of dollars to create a pen that would write in a zero-gravity environment. The Russians (who did not have the huge budget the US had) solved the problem by sending their cosmonauts into space with pencils instead of pens! This simple approach saved them millions!

Here's an example of a simple solution I've developed which solves the problem of telemarketers (which seem to call me even though I registered on the "do not call" list). Whenever they call I ask them to hold on for a moment and hand the phone to my 3-year-old daughter who loves to chat with anyone over the phone. Imagine my total amusement when I did this one evening and overheard my daughter explaining in great detail how she had managed to go "pooh-pooh all by herself that day!" She then told me that the phone was making a strange sound and I listened and heard a dial-tone. Problem solved!

This sort of unconventional thinking might also apply to your retirement. We have been sold the idea that we need to find ways to save and invest enormous sums of money in order to live a comfortable retirement. But realize that the companies that sell you investment products are in business to make money – and the more products they sell you, the more money they make!

One of the key factors that allowed me to retire at 34 is that I questioned conventional "wisdom". I created a plan that benefitted me – ignoring more traditional advice. The common question many people often ask is, "How much money do I need to retire?" Think about that question for a moment – what is your answer? If you're like most people, you will answer this question with a huge lump sum such as, "I need at least $1 million to retire."

The next question I have for you is this, "How much money do you need to live on right now?" When you answer this question, you will probably think you need a certain amount of *income* such as, "I need $50,000 per year." or "I need $3,000 per month."

Why should you measure how much money you need to retire differently than how you measure what you need to live on today? It's crazy! The idea that you need a huge fixed sum of money to retire has been programmed into us – but in truth *you need a dependable* **income** *to live in retirement.* If you have a dependable income, your financial worries evaporate.

Let's use a fictional example to explain this idea of having a stream of income versus the conventional approach of having a large pool of money – and see how the income approach will reduce worries. In this example, water will represent money, and the water will be difficult to get (just as additional income might be difficult to obtain after you stop working)...

Suppose a farmer lives in a very dry area with virtually no rainfall. He has the option of growing crops in two different locations. The first location is next to a large reservoir of water. He can grow crops every year and use the water from the reservoir to water his crops. Even if the reservoir is extremely large, the fact that there is little rainfall adding to the reservoir would mean that he would notice the water level getting lower year after year. As the water continues to be used up, stress and worry would creep into his mind. Taking more water out than the amount that is being replaced is the road to eventual ruin! Isn't it the same with retirement? Plans that tell you to withdraw a certain amount of your nest egg over time can cause stress – because you see your portfolio disappearing over time. You're worried about running out of money! Similarly in this example, the farmer is worried about running out of water.

Suppose there is another location which has a rather small stream. Perhaps the amount of water from the stream is just enough to water the farmer's crops – with very little left over. Suppose the flow of the stream comes from melting snow in the mountains and the water flow is dependable year after year. In this case, the farmer is NOT worried about running out of water. It's the same with financially planning your retirement. If you have a reliable stream of income, you will be much less worried than if you are relying on a large pot of money which isn't growing enough to cover your costs of living.

This is the reason why I will focus on investment tools that provide you with a dependable income in the financial toolbox section of this book. The key point is:

To retire, you need enough INCOME to cover your expenses every year. A huge lump sum should NOT be your focus.

Let's take a moment and step back and look at your situation. To reach a fulfilling retirement, you will need a reasonable amount of money to fulfill wishes and dreams but many of your current expenses will also disappear. In addition, you will probably have other sources of income such as basic government pensions, so you will probably not need to fund your whole retirement with your own resources. For example, let's take a quick look at my situation.

I started saving and investing while attending high school and had built up a fairly sizeable portfolio by the time I entered my 30s. Around that time I started thinking about the whole idea of working for a living. I came to the conclusion that working interferes with my free time – so I developed a plan and left the rat race. When I took the unconventional path of quitting the rat race at 34, I looked at many different financial aspects and I strongly felt that I did not need *anywhere close* to the traditional income that I often hear mentioned. Here's a basic outline of my lifestyle (and how much it costs)…

I am married and we have 5 children (and kids are costly – but I've found not as costly as the "experts" would have you believe). We live mortgage-free in a 4-bedroom, 4-bathroom house in the suburbs of Ottawa. We have a Toyota Sienna minivan and a camping trailer we use during the summertime. Since retiring, we have been to Korea (where my wife is originally from) once, have visited Florida a couple of times during the winter months, and have also taken numerous family trips within Canada – to the east coast and PEI and also out west. This lifestyle has cost us less than $40,000 per year – which seems borderline poverty for a family of seven. How do we do it?

First off, since neither my wife nor I work regular jobs, a lot of the expenses most people face are not part of our budget. We don't have to pay commuting costs, child care costs, parking fees, etc. The simple truth is working is expensive, but once you retire, a lot of your work-related costs simply disappear. In addition, since investment income is tax-advantaged, my tax bill (which for many people is their largest expense) is quite small. Since we only need one vehicle, we save thousands of dollars a year that a second vehicle would cost. Since we have a lot more time than people who work full time, we don't eat out very often. I could go on and on, but the reality is that once you stop working, you might notice a lot of your expenses simply disappear.

I am NOT talking about reducing your spending on all the things you enjoy in life – but reducing work-related costs *should not affect your happiness.* I went into detail about how to simplify your spending without giving things up in chapter 14 of my very first book, *STOP WORKING: Here's How You Can!* The point I am trying to make is that you might need much less money once you retire than what you need now. Remember:

> *Once you retire, a LOT of the expenses you faced while working simply "disappear". This leaves you with more money to spend on things that improve your life.*

This book is a guide for you to realistically plan your exit from the 9-5 grind and live in comfort. In order to do that, the first step is to get a snapshot of your current expenses and income. You will be able to do that in the next section.

Part II

———

CAMERA!

SPENDING YOUR
WAY TO POVERTY?

———

*"Success will never be a big step in the
future; success is a small step now."*
Jonathan Martensson

In this section, we will take a series of snap-
shots of spending and saving ideas. The very
first thing we will look at is your spending versus your income...Take a few minutes to complete this chart:

YOUR Financial Snapshot...TODAY!

Current Expenses	Monthly Cost
HOUSING	
Mortgage/Rent	_____
Line of Credit	_____
Property Taxes	_____
Insurance	_____
Maintenance	_____
Electricity	_____
Gas/Heating	_____
Water	_____
Home Phone	_____
Cell Phone	_____
Cable/Satellite	_____
Internet	_____
Other housing expenses	_____
Total housing expenses	_____ ➔ _____

Current Expenses	Monthly Cost
TRANSPORTATION	
Car #1 Loan/Lease	_____
Car #2 Loan/Lease	_____
Other Cars Loan/Lease	_____
Gas (all cars)	_____
Insurances (all cars)	_____
Maintenance (all cars)	_____
Parking costs	_____
Public Transportation	_____
Total transportation expenses	_____ ➔ _____
FOOD	
Groceries	_____
Dining Out	_____
Quick Food (Coffee, Muffins, etc)	_____
Total Food Costs	_____ ➔ _____

Current Expenses	Monthly Cost
OTHER EXPENSES	
Child Care	_____
School Tuition	_____
Entertainment	_____
Hair/Beauty Services	_____
Club Memberships	_____
Clothing	_____
Gifts	_____
Medical Costs (prescriptions, etc)	_____
Vacations	_____
Other Insurance (Life, Pet, etc)	_____
Pet care costs	_____
Subscriptions (magazines, etc)	_____
Debt Payments (credit cards, etc)	_____

Current Expenses	Monthly Cost
OTHER	
(anything not listed)	_____
	_____
	_____
	_____
Total Other Expenses	_____ → _____
TOTAL EXPENSES	_____

Now you have listed all your current expenses. It is right there in black and white. If you did this exercise with care and did the proper checking, you have concrete numbers to go by.

Once you've figured out your current expenses, you need calculate your income. Calculating your current income should be relatively easy – as shown on next page. Simply fill in the chart to get a complete picture of your *after-tax* income:

Current Income	Monthly Amount
Take-Home Pay (after taxes, etc.)	_____
Spouses Take-Home Pay (after tax, etc)	_____
* Rental Income (investment property)	_____
* Investment Income (stocks, bonds, etc.)	_____
Pension Income	_____
Other Income	_____
Other Income	_____
Other Income	_____
TOTAL INCOME	_____

* Note that rental income and investment income means actual income (not capital gains or price appreciation). For rental income, this means net rental income after expenses such as taxes, repairs, mortgage payments and an allowance for the fact that the property might be vacant from time to time. Investment income would include dividends and interest payments that you receive and that you expect to continue into the future. You will need to see how much tax you are paying on these sources of income to figure out your after-tax income. If you don't

know how to calculate these amounts, you can look it up in *"Your Personal Tax Planning Guide"* which is a FREE guide available at many major libraries. This guide is created by the Certified General Accountants (CGAs) of Ontario. You could also look at your income tax forms and figure out how much tax you pay or you could ask your accountant.

Once you have calculated your current net income, you can compare it to your current expenses to see what your current surplus is (or deficit if you spend more than you earn). This gives you a very good starting point to plan for your retirement.

CURRENT INCOME AND EXPENSES

This is the money you have coming in versus how much you are spending. Unless you are facing an unforeseen event such as a job loss, this number (current income minus current expenses) should be positive (in other words the money coming in should be higher than the money going out). If this is your situation, you can skip ahead to the next chapter.

If you are not facing a temporary problem and you are spending more than you earn, you have to take immediate action. This situation will cause you undue stress and can lead to dire financial straits down the road. Here's what you should do right now. Go back to your worksheet and take a red pen and circle all your wants (i.e. such as the Tim Horton's coffee you purchase each morning) and NOT needs (i.e. mortgage, heat, and hydro). Once you have a number of your wants circled, take out a piece of scrap paper and list them all in a ranked order from your favourite to your least favourite with their respective dollar amounts. When you've finished this short exercise you will have an idea of where your money is going.

Review your financial snapshot in the current income and expenses area. Write down exactly by how much your expenses are higher than your income on the same scrap piece of paper where you ranked your list of wants. This number is your current spending deficit. Now take the lowest ranked want from your list and subtract it from this deficit. If the number becomes zero or negative you can stop. If not, keep repeating this process taking your least favourite want and subtracting it from your number until you reach zero (or below zero).

Here's a hypothetical example to show you:
Suppose your current monthly financial situation looked like this:

1) Total Current Income	$ 4,850
2) Total Current Expenses	$ 5,150
Surplus or Deficit ($4,850 minus $5,150)	–$ 300

As you can see from the above calculation, you are spending $300 a month more than you are earning. This is something you would have to fix if you wanted to have comfort in retirement.

Let's assume you looked at your expenses and circled all your wants with a red pen. Then you listed these on a separate scrap piece of paper so that they are listed in order of your favourite to least favourite expenses:

Internet	$ 40
Vacations	$150
Club Memberships	$ 50
Gifts	$100
Entertainment	$100
Cable/Satellite	$ 75
Dining Out	$150
Quick Food (Coffee, Muffins, etc)	$ 60
Clothing	$150
Cell Phone	$ 60
Subscriptions (magazines, etc.)	$ 50

From the information, you can see that your least favourite unnecessary expense includes some magazine subscriptions costing $50 per month. Perhaps these are old subscriptions that you have never bothered cancelling. In a few minutes you can quickly reduce your spending by $50/month or $600/year.

Here's how your spending deficit would look after cancelling the subscriptions:

Spending Deficit	$300
Less: Savings from cancelled subscription	−$50
New Spending deficit	$250

You've now reduced your spending by $50/month but you are still spending $250 more than you earn every month. The next item on your list is your cell phone. In real life you might need your cell phone, but in this example, we assume you don't really. In this case, if you cancel the service, your deficit would be:

Spending Deficit	$250
Less: Savings from cancelled cell phone	$ 60
New Spending deficit	$ 190

You still need to eliminate $190 of spending per month. The next item on your list is clothing at $150 per month. Obviously you need some clothing, but perhaps you could reduce your spending to $75 per month.

This $75 saving would bring your spending deficit down to $190 minus $75 = $115. You would keep going up the list and eliminating or reducing expenses until you brought your deficit to zero. Once you complete this exercise, you will no longer be spending more than you earn every month. If you can cut your expenses a little more, you will create extra money which can then be directed towards saving and investing for your future.

Now that you know your current spending versus your income and you are not spending more than you earn, let's take a look at your possible retirement spending and how you might be able to spend less while not giving anything up...

Finishing Your Vegetables BEFORE Enjoying Dessert!

"If you would be wealthy, think of saving as well as getting."

Benjamin Franklin

I confess to having a bit of a sweet tooth and I really look forward to dessert. I like some vegetables and despise others. However, as an adult, you probably eat your veggies before moving onto dessert – because it's good for you. Well the reality is that most people would rather earn more money than reduce spending. That's reasonable because if you can painlessly earn more money, why not? But the reality is that controlling spending is probably much more firmly in your control than earning more (especially through investing). In addition, every dollar saved is much more powerful than an extra dollar earned, because every dollar saved is an *after-tax dollar.* If you earn an extra dollar, the reality is that you only get to keep 60-70 cents *after paying the income tax.* With this fact in mind, let's take a look at your costs first. Are there ways that you can reduce your spending *without* living the miserly existence similar to that of the famed Ebenezer Scrooge?

Take a quick look at your expenses in the previous chapter. The very first item you should look at would be debt payments. If you have any debt, you should make a plan to eliminate it! With finances (and most other things in life), it's often better to deal with the "known" before the "unknown". Paying off debt is totally risk-free. There is no risk of a sudden financial catastrophe derailing your plans with debt repayment. Once a debt is gone – it's gone! In my book, *"STOP WORKING TOO: You Still Can!"* I dedicated an entire chapter to debt. An example I gave supposes someone went into a store and purchased a $3,000 big-screen TV and charged it on their credit cards. In the example, if they only made the minimum payments every month (and NEVER charged anything else on their card), it would take them 22 years to pay the entire amount off! In addition, the total cost would jump from $3,000 to over $7,000 with credit card interest charges being what they are. I entitled the chapter, *"From Debtors Prisons to Wage Slavery"* because paying for a purchase for 22 years seems to me like a sort of debt prison sentence and too many of these claims on your money will turn you into a perpetual wage slave. So pay off *ALL* your debts before you retire. Okay – enough with the sermon, let's move on...

The other huge debt item you need to look at is your mortgage (and other housing costs for that matter). I understand many people have an emotional attachment to their homes because they have so many memories there. However, if the kids are gone and you are shuffling around in a massive Mcmansion that takes a tremendous effort to clean and maintain (not to mention all the expenses related to owning a larger house) you might look at downsizing. In one quick move, you might be able to pay off your mortgage immediately or pocket a huge windfall if you are already mortgage-free. This extra money might be enough to fund a huge portion of your retirement income needs– by increasing your future expected income without you being forced to pinch pennies so hard that your thumbs begin to hurt. As an added bonus, with a smaller house, your expenses such as taxes, maintenance, and utilities are also likely to fall (which means your expenses also fall). This one move helps you in two ways – it reduces your expenses while at the same time possibly giving you extra money to invest which can increase your overall income!

These two quick moves of eliminating debt and downsizing might be substantial enough all on their own for you to bring your future expenses in line with your future income. If not, look at the other expenses. Will you need two cars if you and your spouse are both retired? Will you really need a cell phone? Look at all your expenses and figure out which ones you could cut *without hurting your lifestyle!* The truth is – you want to enjoy life too. These numbers can put plugged into the chart in the retirement action workbook at the back of this book.

*Remember – you are trying to cut the
expenses that don't add to your happiness – NOT cut your happiness so that
you don't add to your expenses!*

I am not impressed when I hear financial advice about simply cutting back on buying a morning cup of coffee or never dining out to save money. What if you like coffee or dining out? Also forget budgeting for most people – the reality is that *budgeting is NOT fun and most people won't stick to a budget.* I prefer to divide my expenses into life-enhancing and non life-enhancing. Then I focus my efforts on cutting out (or reducing the costs of) the things that don't add any value to my life. For example, I do everything possible to legally minimize my taxes because I have never looked at my taxes as a life-enhancing event. Think about it...we all know that we collectively need to pay a certain amount of taxes to maintain certain services we all value – but the truth is that the amount you pay in taxes is not related at all to the level of services you personally receive. There are no special libraries or hospitals for high tax payers. The reality is that Canada is a highly taxed country. This is the reason there are thousands of professional accountants employed for the purpose of reducing their clients' tax burdens. Therefore, since paying more tax than I have to will not enhance my life in any way, I use basic tax planning and other tools such as RRSPs and TFSAs (tax-free savings accounts) to reduce my tax bill wherever possible. So taxes are non life-enhancing expenses.

In contrast I am not willing to forgo family trips because they are fun. These trips help build memories and they are important to me – so I wouldn't dream of cutting them out in order to save a few extra bucks. If something enhances your life, why would you want to cut it out?

The general idea is that you should focus on reducing non life-enhancing expenses as much as possible. Even seemingly small expenses add up. You also have to look at what's life-enhancing to you. To see the power of this approach, here's a real-life example. After giving a talk at an area university, I did a quick calculation with a student who was paying around $60/month for his cell phone service and discovered that this one item will cost him around $100,000 over his lifetime. Is that worth it? It might be to him – but it's not to me. A cell phone would not improve my life one iota – I would rather have the extra $100,000.

Many people feel they must buy certain trinkets because "everyone else has one". By avoiding that trap – you can save huge sums of money. Don't let useless trinkets affect your plans for retirement.

Saving money by spending wisely seems boring – but it makes a huge difference over time. Another personal example occurred when I graduated from university in the early 1990s. Around that time the economy was terrible and the only job I could find was a minimum wage retail clerk job. I made a grand total of around $6/hour (which works out to around $12,000/ year). Even in the early 90s, this was not a lot of money. However, I had dreamt of going to Australia and New Zealand for a number of years so I turned my efforts with laser focus to saving for that goal – and I did end up spending an entire wonderful year there. But while I was saving for this life-enhancing goal, I focused my attention on reducing or eliminating things that did not improve my life. One of the items that got my attention was bank fees.

At this time there were no internet banking institutions such as ING direct or PC Financial. Since there was little competition, the big banks had been very aggressive with increasing their banking fees. At that time I had a "grandfathered" account where I did not have to pay a monthly fee – but I was limited to two free transactions every month (after which I was charged something like $1-$2 for every cheque written or withdrawal made). The bank also charged $20-$30 if you ordered a book of cheques! With various bills I had to pay and cheques I had to write, this account was going to cost me $10-$20 per month). I know this amount seems small – but that works out to $120-$240 per year. Let's take a quick moment to think about that. Remember at that time I was only earning a measly $6 per hour, so this one expense would cost me 20-40 work hours per year! I would be working up to an entire week just to pay for bank fees!

So here's what I did. I had a Visa card which also offered Visa cheques (which charged high interest rates, but no fees). The trick was if your

Visa card had a positive balance, you were never charged any interest when writing a cheque. Every time my paycheque was deposited into my bank account I would immediately transfer most of it to my Visa card and then pay all my bills with Visa cheques. This way I avoided all the bank fees since there would only be one trans-action per pay period. I used this system for 5-6 years (before fee-free internet banks appeared), so in total this one move saved me close to $1,000 of fees and the cost of cheques – and it was not inconvenient at all.

If you think about your expenses while you are working, you realize your biggest expense is taxes. Once you retire and your income drops, your tax bill drops considerably. The next largest expense for many people is the mortgage payment – but if you've paid off your mortgage (or plan to down-size to kill your mortgage), that is another huge expense that simply vanishes. Other work-related deductions such as CPP, EI, or pension payments also vanish. Parking and other commuting costs also disappear. In addition, since you are now retired, the costs of saving for retirement are also gone. These are the expenses I predicted would vanish when I stopped working seven years ago – but it gets better.

There is a common expression that "Time is Money". Generally this means that if you are using your time, you should get paid for it in some way. Well another thing I've noticed since I left the rat race is that I can choose to do things when they're cheap to do. For example, go-carting is half price on Tuesdays during the day. If I worked at the regular 9-5 grind, it would be hard to bring the kids at that time. Since I don't work I can go during the day on Tuesdays and save a lot of money. Same thing with movies – the regular price for a show is $11 per adult and $8 per child. Since I have four children (and a baby), the cost for the family would be $54 (without popcorn)! But we've found a few specials during March Break and other school holidays where admission was as cheap as $2 each (so $12 instead of $54). The list of savings goes on and on – if your time is flexible. My point is that once you retire, you will have more time and you will be able to be more strategic when buying things (without going to extremes).

If you are retiring at a more traditional age, some of your costs will fall due to senior discounts. A quick check of the internet shows discounts of 25-35% for many simple purchases – such as movie tickets, museum admission, fitness memberships and even some consumer products. Some city transit services even offer free seniors days and/or significant discounts. The point is that you can find ways to save money without giving anything up. Be creative – it's well worth the effort in many cases. I understand that you don't want to spend your life chasing deals, but a few minor adjustments can make a huge difference. Now let's move on to looking at ways to increase your estimated retirement income.

Is "Work" a Four-Letter Word?

———

"I always arrive late at the office, but I make up for it by leaving early."
Charles Lamb

Do you like your job? If you do, the easiest way to add to your retirement funding is to work an extra few years. The recent trend for some soon-to-be retirees is to work a little longer. This move can give a tremendous boost to your finances for two reasons. First, while you are working, you are not drawing on your pension or other assets so they are able to continue growing for you. Second, if you have excess income while working, you might be in the position to save some of your income to top up your retirement funds or pay off some debts.

Studies have also shown that working is good for your health as it can provide you with extra socialization and add meaning to your life. This seems to be true as many retirees want to be engaged and productive – which is why the majority of volunteers are seniors. One of the interesting things I've noticed is that the happiest people in the world are those engaged in an activity which totally captures their attention and interest. Think of the stereotypical researcher getting close to a major breakthrough – all other things in his life seem unimportant.

My life has been incredibly enriched since I decided to write financial books and do public speaking. This is going to sound like huge contradiction but I love working and want to keep working until the day I die. A reasonable question you might ask then is, "Why did you retire at 34?" The answer is simple but took me a while to realize – if you are doing something you enjoy, working really does add more meaning to life. BUT, just like anything else, there are some good things and some bad things about working. In my own case, I write books and do public speaking about a topic I am passionate about – personal finance. I truly find new information interesting. However, having a boss telling me what to do, waking up to the obnoxious sound of an alarm clock every morning, fighting slow-moving rush hour traffic, having time deadlines, being force to do things I find pointless or stupid – all these factors are negatives I refuse to put up with since I stopped working. I have escaped the rat race but still enjoy working at what I do...but on my own terms. If you enjoy what you do, why stop early?

What if you hate your job and can't wait to end it? In this case, of course you might want to retire as soon as possible. But does that mean you want to totally stop working? Whenever I go to The Home Depot to pick up something for my house, I can't help noticing a lot of older people working there. I've spoken with a couple of them at my local store and they told me they enjoy doing it – they started working there after their careers had finished. They work part-time – which allows them to do what they enjoy while also earning a few extra dollars. Many people who had high-powered careers enjoy doing something totally different once they end their careers.

I learned this fact at one of the most interesting classes I took in university. The course was called Entrepreneurship and the professor invited real business owners to the class regularly. I remember a fellow came in who owned a fairly large Ottawa-based flower shop business. He explained his business in detail (which sounds boring but was actually quite interesting) and at the end he asked if anyone had any questions. One of the students then asked if he was hiring at the time and he responded that he only hired older people because they were the most reliable workers. Then he told us a story of one of his employees – his former accountant. This guy had become a partner at a local accounting firm and became extremely wealthy. After retiring, he was bored so he then started delivering flowers. He enjoyed the interaction and everyone was always happy whenever he delivered flowers – so he *really* enjoyed it. He didn't need the money he just did it for the fun of it. It's the same thing for many people who volunteer – they do it because they *want* to... Whether you want to work at something completely different is up to you.

Just for interest, here is one other example of a person who preferred working to retirement – her name was Rose Bumpkin. She immigrated to the US from Russia (where she had been born in 1893) and opened a furniture store in Omaha Nebraska with $500 called Nebraska Furniture Mart with a very simple business plan: "*Sell Cheap and Tell the Truth*". Then in 1983, Warren Buffett (one of the richest men in the world) wanted to buy her store so he agreed to pay $55 million for 80% of her business (and $55 million was a lot of money in 1983)! After the deal was finalized, she went home. The next day before the store opened, she was right there ready to continue managing the store. She kept on working at the store - zipping around in her motorized cart (she was 90 years old at that time). Then a few years later, at the age of 95, she had an argument about how the carpeting department should be run, so she promptly quit and opened another store called Mrs. B's Warehouse a short distance away from Nebraska Furniture Mart – and apparently made a sizeable dent in their business. A few years later, she reconciled and sold her new business back to Warren Buffett for another $5 million and went back to work at her original store. She worked right up to a few months before her death at 104.

For some people working is a necessary evil and escape is all they can think about. For others, working is what they love to do. So ask yourself, "Is work a four-letter word you'd pre-fer to avoid, or not?" Even if you quit what you are doing now, you can still move into some-thing you enjoy doing part-time. Also be aware that with recent changes to legislation, you can start collecting CPP and also keep working at the same time. This added twist might be of interest to you.

Now let's move on and take a look at some income you might be eligible for – you just have to ask for it.

YOU SEE $20 ON THE SIDEWALK... DO YOU PICK IT UP?

"The do-it-yourself version of pensions is a flop, as many have painfully learned"

- William Greider

Warren Buffett, one of the world's richest men, was once seen picking up a penny on an elevator and remarked to the stunned witness, "The beginning of the next billion." I've ignored many pennies I've seen on the ground over the years, but I would stop and bend down to pick up $20. Would you? You might be thinking, "What does this have to do with planning for retirement?"

A lot!

According to Canada's Task Force on Financial Literacy, thousands of people are simply "ignoring" thousands of dollars just sitting there for the taking. In a report released in early 2011, it was revealed that around 55,000 people are missing out on Canada Pension Plan (CPP) – benefits that they have paid into. Around 160,000 people who are eligible to receive Old Age Security (OAS) have neglected to apply for it. An additional 135,000-150,000 are missing out on Guaranteed Income Supplement (GIS) benefits. Forget picking up measly pennies – these government benefits can be worth thousands of dollars!

Make sure to apply for any government benefits you are entitled to. If you don't know if you are eligible – find out!

Taxpayers must apply for these benefits in order to receive them and many people are failing to do this. Not applying is like ignoring $100 bills just lying on the sidewalk as you take a stroll. In addition, if you apply too late, you won't get all the benefits you missed because retroactive payments are limited to 11 months in most cases.

I wrote about CPP and OAS extensively in my book, *STOP WORKING TOO: You Still Can!*. Many people are under the assumption that CPP and OAS will not be there for them when they retire. Historically CPP was structured to be a "pay as you go" plan where current workers' contributions funded current retirees' pensions. This idea works very well if you have an ever-increasing population, but the whole model can fall apart if you have a large generation followed by a smaller generation (such as with the baby boomers followed by the Gen Xers). With this fact being very clear a long time ago, the government in the 1990s made some changes to the plan. The first step was to increase contribution rates. The idea was to build up a fund that would pay retirees once the boomers started retiring on a large scale. In addition, the Canada Pension Plan Investment Board was created to manage this pool of money with the idea that over time, the fund could earn a better rate of return which would help grow the assets for when they are needed. Actuarial estimates have stated that the CPP is on stable footing for decades to come. The main message is that CPP will probably be there when you need it – but there will probably be some minor tweaks over time.

To get an estimate of how much CPP you can expect to receive, call 1-800-277-9914. There you will be guided through a series of prompts, but if you hit zero after a few prompts, you can speak to a person who can help you. From there you can ask for an estimate of your future pension. The whole process takes about 5 minutes. This office will give you approximate figure based on historical contributions and you can add various different scenarios that might apply to your personal circumstances and they will do the calculations for you.

As for Old Age Security (OAS), there are no individual accounts and there is no OAS "fund". Payments are made from general government revenues to everyone over the age of 65 who has lived in Canada for 10 years or more. In order to get the full benefit, the requirement is for you to have lived in Canada for at least 40 years. The benefit is prorated if you lived in Canada less than 40 years. In addition, the benefit gets clawed back if you have a high income. The most recent clawback rules for 2011 indicate that 15% of your benefit is clawed back for any income over $67,668. There is some risk of OAS being reduced in the future if governments face funding pressures, but because this is a senior's benefit (and seniors vote in larger numbers); governments will be very hesitant to cut this program.

There is also another program called the Guaranteed Income Supplement (GIS) which provides a monthly non-taxable income to some people. This is a benefit available to lower income seniors. To receive this benefit, you must apply for it (and many people lose out because they are not aware of this fact). There are a lot of variables that go into the calculation of this benefit, so I won't get into all these variables here.

If you would like to see more information about OAS and/or GIS, go to *www.service-canada.gc.ca* and click on *retirement planning* on the left-hand side of the screen. Then simply scroll down until you see the headings "Old Age Security" or "Guaranteed Income Supplement". You can also find out more about the Canada Pension Plan at this site.

Also be aware that you can take CPP earlier or later than age 65, but this option would reduce the amount you're entitled to by 0.6% for each month earlier than your 65th birthday.

For example, if you took it at age 60, your pension would be reduced by:

0.6% X 60 months = 36% LESS

By taking CPP at age 60, your pension amount would be reduced by 36%.

For example, if your regular CPP pension is $500/month but you decide to take it at age 60 instead of age 65, you would receive:

$500 (regular CPP pension) minus 36% = $320/month

Conversely, if you decided to take your pension later, you would earn 0.7% more each year until the age of 70. So if you took your pension at age 70, you would earn:

0.7% X 60 months = 42% MORE

As an example once again, if your regular CPP is $500/month and you delay taking it until age 70, your pension income would be:

$500 (regular CPP pension) plus 42% = $710/month

An entire book could be written on the various aspects of CPP and OAS alone, but that would get away from the purpose of this book which is a more holistic look at YOUR retirement – but you should know how this plan works. If you want to look at the cost/benefits of taking CPP either early or late, or you simply want to learn a lot more about how the plan is administered, I would suggest you use information that is available to you online. Go to www.retirehappyblog.ca and type "CPP" in the search heading. Here you will find a variety of articles to help you learn more about CPP. In addition, if you'd like to find out more about Old Age Security, go to www.retirehappyblog.ca and type "OAS" in the search column and you will see numerous articles.

Even if you don't have a defined employee pension plan, you might still be able to create a reasonable retirement with combined CPP/OAS benefits and perhaps a little extra savings. To get an idea of how this would all come together for you, read my previous book, *STOP WORKING TOO: You Still Can!* (from pages 35-61).

These plans provide safe, reliable income which is mostly indexed to inflation. These simple benefits can provide you with a solid foundation on which to build your worry-free retirement.

Your Financial Toolbox...Which Tools Do YOU Need?

"If you wait to do everything until you're sure it's right, you'll probably never do much of anything."
Win Borden

If you've ever done a home repair, worked on your car, or even assemble furniture, you have probably used a variety of tools. It would be completely silly for someone to come up to you and tell you for example that a hammer is much better than a screwdriver or you should always use a wrench instead of a saw. The reality is that every tool in your toolbox serves a specific function. If you need to cut a piece of wood, trying to use a screwdriver or hammer to do it would be ridiculous. It is completely obvious even to an average 5-year-old that you need a saw to cut wood.

It's the same with investment products. One type of investment is not necessarily better than the other. Just like tools in a toolbox, which financial tools you choose depends on what you are trying to accomplish. Keep in mind that every financial tool serves a different purpose. I will explain how some tools can work for you a little later, but before we do that, let's take a look at the risks you face (so that you know how to protect yourself against them).

YOUR RETIREMENT RISKS...

1. Running out of money:
One of the biggest worries many retirees face is the prospect of running out of money in retirement. Think about it – you save up for your entire working life and then start enjoying retirement and then a decade or so down the road you realize that you are broke – not

a desirable fate. The Canada Pension Plan and Old Age Security along with the Guaranteed Income Supplement (if you're eligible) provide most retires with a basic income for life but in many cases you probably want a higher income. The tools that might help in this area would be an extra supplemental pension or various annuities which we'll look at a little later.

2. Inflation eating away at your spending power:

I remember a number of years ago hearing an elderly fellow explain to me how many people wanted to work for the railroads when he graduated because, "They paid a solid $100 per month pension." What would $100/month provide you with today? The reality is that inflation has taken a huge bite out of your purchasing power over time. For interest I Googled the prices for various goods in 1960. The information I found was for the US, but Canadian prices would be similar:

Cost of an average house:	$16,500
Cost of a Gallon of Gas:	31 cents
Cost of mailing a letter:	4 cents

Prices have risen A LOT since then and they should keep on rising. Once again, CPP, OAS, and GIS are all increased annually roughly in line with the increase in some prices, so a base amount of your income is covered. However, most investments you might choose on your own do not protect you against inflation over time with the exception of quality, blue-chip stocks and real estate.

3. **Financial Crisis/Stock Market Crash:**
   The reason why most retirees do not put all their money into stocks is because they fear a potential panic or selloff wiping out a huge portion of their savings. Many more conservative investments protect you against this such as bonds, GICs, annuities, and other investments from solid companies that pay you regular interest. The reality is that stock markets are unpredictable – you never know when the next financial panic might happen. However, if you rely on solid dividend stocks

for income, the stock market volatility is less of a factor for you. Still, most older investors would never put all their money into stocks.

4. Financial Protection of Family Members:

Another factor you want to make sure of is that your loved ones are taken care of if something happens to you. By the time you are nearing retirement, the main concern for most people will be their spouse (as the kids are usually grown up and on their own by this time). You might want to do proper estate and tax planning and also familiarize yourself with your pension spousal benefits (which is beyond the scope of this book) but still worthy of your consideration.

5. Unforeseen Financial Calamity

You never know if you might face some unexpected event and need some cash very quickly. It's always good to have some cash on hand that is easy to access quickly. To do this, you might want to set aside a small portion of your investments into savings accounts or other short term deposits so you will have access to ready cash in case of an emergency. For this money a simple savings account will do.

Now that we have looked at some of the potential risks you might face, let's look at the financial tools that are available to you...

1. STOCKS

Let me be very clear on this – I love stocks and I love the stock market. To fully understand the wealth creation power of partial ownership in companies (which is essentially what stocks are), I would like to use my personal life as an example. After graduation, I made almost all the wrong moves as far as securing my financial future. I spent a summer backpacking around Europe then followed that up with a year in Australia and New Zealand. After that, I moved from Ottawa to Vancouver and got a job at BC Tel (a forerunner to Telus) where some advancement opportunities existed. But shortly thereafter I quit and went to East Asia to teach. After getting married, my wife and I decided we wanted a large family (by today's standards) and had five kids. And during this whole time, I never embarked on a real career – I merely had a series of jobs that paid the bills. Every single one of these moves, although VERY enriching from a life experience point of view, was the wrong move from a financial point of view.

But I did one important thing right...I saved as much as I could and with that money I always bought stocks. I never bought a tech stock or other fast-growing company, but stuck with boring companies that had been in business at least 100 years or more – companies like the big banks in Canada, Coca-Cola, Johnson and Johnson, Enbridge, etc.

Simple thought...Stocks, like wine, tend to get better with age. You can save yourself a lot of grief if you only buy stocks that have been in business a century or more.

In my late 20s my parents began to worry a little and ask me what I planned to do with my life. I told them I was not sure but I was not worried because my portfolio kept growing. Then in 2000 when the technology stock bubble imploded and countless investors lost a bundle of money on stocks such as Nortel and JDS Uniphase, my boring strategy really paid off.

The National Post did an article about my investment portfolio – which had grown to over $250,000 by that time. A few years later at the age of 34, I quit the rat race. In my late 30s my net worth surpassed the $1 million mark. The stock market has been very rewarding

The point of telling you this is to show the extreme power of wealth creation of the stock market over time *if you invest properly*. I call myself *The Idiot Millionaire* because I did *nothing* spectacular in my life as it relates to making money – but the great companies I invested in did great things for me. My point is that it is extremely difficult to build wealth if you completely ignore the stock market but if you invest some money in good quality, dividend-paying stocks, you will be rewarded over time.

I am very biased towards stocks because my experience with them has been mostly good. If you are older and need to be more conservative, you probably don't want to invest all your money into the stock market but investing a portion into dividend-paying stocks makes a lot of sense. The older you are, the less you probably want to invest in stocks because the stock market goes up and down like a yo-yo in the short-term (the "short-term" is 10 years or less).

But people are living longer than previous generations, so many people should aim to have a portion of their assets continuing to grow even after they retire. To control risk, DON'T take unnecessary gambles with new companies with a lot of promise but not much of a track record. Stick to companies that have been in business for decades and have a long history of paying increasing dividends – like the list of stocks I provided in my book, *"The Idiot Millionaire"*.

You might have had some really bad experiences with stocks and might have sworn off them forever. If this is you, I can understand and maybe you need to continue with this idea. The truth is a good night's sleep is priceless and if investing in the stock market keeps you up at night, then it is not something you should do. Just realize that by choosing this option, you'll probably end up with more sleep and less money over time – which might be a reasonable trade-off.

However if you need some of the growth stocks offer but can't afford to lose money, you could use the strategy outlined on pages 99-110 in my book, *STOP WORKING TOO: You Still Can!* (the chapter entitled, *Invest in Stocks and NEVER Lose Money – Guaranteed!*). This strategy allows you to still reap some of the rewards of stock ownership without taking on the risk of losing your money. It would be tedious and time-consuming to repeat the whole approach here, but it involves using strip bonds (which are explained) to cover potential stock losses.

Numerous studies have shown stocks to be the best investment for wealth creation so once again – having a portion of your assets in stocks might be a good idea.

Pros:

Usually protects you from inflation over time and is also a great wealth creator.

Cons:

Can be volatile which is not ideal for people who may need to access their money. If you don't stick with super quality companies that have been in business for decades, severe problems or even bankruptcy can happen.

2. REAL ESTATE

The other investment which has made many people rich is real estate. Most people who have bought a home at some point in their lives have seen the value increase. The majority of Canadians own their own home because as they gradually pay off their mortgage they own a bigger slice of their house until one day it's completely paid off. Once you are mortgage-free, a large part of your living costs disappear. In addition, since people are not tempted to buy and sell their houses at a click of a mouse (like many do with stocks), most people who have purchased houses over the years have done well.

Investment real estate is a little different in that you are trying to generate an income. The big benefit of using this approach is that you are buying something you can see and feel. You know it's there and you can see what you're buying (many people do not have a clue about the stocks they are buying). In addition, you can often put a small portion of the cost of the property down and then finance the rest with a mortgage and then make the payments with the rental income you are collecting. This has been done successfully by a lot of people over the years.

A number of years ago I worked at my Dad's used appliance store and working there allowed me to meet some interesting people. One part of the business was supplying small landlords with appliances for their units. One day I began speaking with one of these landlords (who was a regular customer of ours) about real estate and he spent a lot of time explaining it to me. He had purchased units in distressed areas of town and managed to buy them cheaply and then upgrade them. Overall he was doing very well, but once we discussed the problems of tenants, I soon decided that real estate also came with many headaches such as unforeseen repairs or difficult tenants. Some people choose to have a property management company handle these problems for them for a fee, but in many cases your success depends on the reliability of the company you choose. Since I am a generally lazy guy who is not keen to face difficult problems regularly, it was around this time that I decided to focus on investing in stocks rather than real estate.

There was one situation in early 2009 when I came very close to investing a substantial amount of money in real estate. I had noticed a property for sale which essentially was a vacant lot beside a triplex. I spoke with the seller's agent a few times but we were unable to reach a deal. The reason I wanted this property (the vacant lot portion), was because the property was located close to an area which had numerous government office buildings with inadequate parking. The land was already being used as a parking lot and generating money every day. This was the ONLY investment in real estate I have ever considered. Think about it...if you have a small parking lot the ONLY required action on your part is the automatic payment machine and clearing the snow in the winter (which can easily be contracted out). You have no tenant legislation, no repairs or maintenance, and you never have to chase people to pay you (if people don't pay their cars get towed). In addition, the majority of parking in Ottawa is run by the city and this is one of their major revenue sources, so prices continue to rise faster than inflation. And the best part – they're not making any more parking spaces because land is limited.

Real estate can be a good investment option for some people, but if you are getting close to retirement and have never owned a rental real estate property before you should probably steer clear of this as there are too many potential issues to deal with. If you want some real estate investments, you might want to look at REITs (which stand for real estate investment trusts). These are investments that own a variety of buildings in many different areas. They collect rent and send you a large portion of the income they generate automatically. So instead of owning a managing one or two properties, you own a small piece of maybe a thousand or two thousand properties.

The main point is that real estate might be something you are familiar with and it is a good tool for generating wealth, but I have always avoided it because it often requires a lot of work and comes with potential headaches.

Pros:

Usually protects you from inflation over time and also is a great wealth creator – especially if you leverage to buy it (borrow money).

Cons:

It can be difficult to sell quickly if you need the money. It can be a burden to collect rent and there can be maintenance issues. Rent controls can be implemented and rules can change over time.

3. BONDS OR GICS

Bonds and GICs (guaranteed investment certifi-cates) are interest-bearing investments which promise you a fixed rate of interest for a certain period of time. Bonds are issued by national, provincial, and municipal governments as well as by corporations. You get a fixed interest rate depending on the general level of interest rates when you purchase the bond and also the level of risk you are willing to assume. For example, if you had purchased a 10-year Government of Canada bond in the early 1980s, you would have received over 12% whereas in 2011, a sim-ilar bond was offering only around 2% – because interest rates have fallen. However, Canada is seen as a low-risk borrower but if you are will-ing to incur more risk by lending to a third

world country for example, you can often get a
higher rate of return.

> *IMPORTANT! If you are buying bonds
> for your retirement, only buy the highest
> quality bonds. Looking for higher yields
> by buying higher risk bonds is not wise
> for your retirement savings. Once you
> retire, return **of** your money becomes
> more important that return **on** your
> money.

Bonds can be a reasonable place to put
some of your money if you are getting closer to
retirement. However, don't invest too much in
bonds (especially today) because if you are
earning around 2% on your bonds, you might
actually be losing money because of inflation.
For example, if prices start rising at 3% or more,
your interest will not keep up.

GICs, which are usually offered by banks,
are similar to bonds in that they pay a fixed rate
of interest. They usually have terms of 1-5
years. Again, this may be a suitable place for
part of your retirement savings but you have to

realize that you are mostly just going to be preserving your wealth rather than increasing it because of inflation. One more important fact is that you can have up to $100,000 invested in GICs at major Canadian banks and that money is CDIC insured – so you can be pretty confident your money is safe.

Note: If you have more than $100,000, you can open accounts at different banks and be insured up to $100,000 at each one.

> ** Remember – When you see GIC rates posted at your bank – these are simply suggested prices. Try to negotiate the interest rate (just as you should do with your mortgage), and if you are a good customer, you will often get a better rate.*

Pros:

If you stick with major banks your money is CDIC insured (up to $100,000). If you stick with quality bonds (such as Canada bonds), you are pretty much guaranteed repayment. You also know exactly how much you'll earn for a set amount of time.

Cons:

These might not keep up with inflation over the long term. With GICs, your money is locked in for a certain time period. With bonds, if you cash out early, you might lose money (depending on interest rate movements).

4. ANNUITIES

Annuities are often overlooked and many people have a negative feeling about them as they are seen as "just another insurance product", but they can be a great tool to help you retire. In this section I will be giving a lot more information about annuities because they are not well understood by a lot of people.

Annuities can create a dependable income stream for you in retirement. In simple terms, an annuity is the exact opposite of a life insurance policy. With a regular life insurance policy you pay a certain amount every month and in the event you die – your beneficiary is entitled to a lump sum. With a standard annuity, you pay a lump sum up front and then receive a regular payment until you die (or a certain length of time, depending on the contract). When you contribute the lump sum amount, the insurance company invests this money in fixed income investments and uses some of the interest they generate to pay you. Immediately you should ask yourself why you should buy an annuity – why not simply buy these fixed income investments the insurance companies invest in and leave it at that?

The reason that you might want to get an annuity is because the rate you get on your money *will actually be higher than the rate of interest your lump sum is earning!* How's this possible? You know insurance companies are in business to make money. How can they pay you more than your money is earning?

The key is that insurance companies look at mortality tables to determine how long (on average) somebody of your age, gender, etc. should live. Then they take into account that some people will pass away earlier while others will pass away later – so payments are shifted accordingly. Let's use a simple example to explain how this works:

Suppose ten elderly people decide to pool their money and invest it in fixed income investments. They each invest $10,000 and the investment earns 5%. They have collectively invested $100,000 in total and that investment earns 5%. Now assume they also agree that anybody who passes away during the year forfeits their share of the pot and that money is redistributed to the other investors. After the first year, assume that one person passes away. Now there is $105,000 ($100,000 initial amount plus 5% interest) which is divided by nine people instead of 10. Now everybody has:

$105,000 divided by 9 = $11,667 each

In this case, they each now have $11,667. This means that they have earned 16.67% on their money! If they had simply invested the money themselves and earned the same 5% rate their money earned in interest, they would only have $10,500 each (their $10,000 investment plus 5%). The reason they earn more income is because one of the contributors has passed away and forfeited his portion of the investment. This is the reason annuities usually provide a much higher rate of return than regular fixed income investments. This bears repeating because it is the foundation upon which annuity returns are built:

> *Those people that don't collect their annuity payments for a long time effectively subsidize those that do! By doing this, you can earn a MUCH higher return on your money and guarantee yourself that you never run out of money.*

Since a large portion of the annuity return is based on this fact, they are more effective the older you are.

Some people are turned off of annuities because they are reluctant to give up control of their money. Let's look at this issue a little more closely...

Do you have a pension plan at work? If not, have you ever looked on with envy at people who are lucky enough to work for an employer which offers a good pension plan? These people contribute to their pensions and give up control of their money in exchange for a guaranteed pension offering a regular income upon retirement. *Buying an annuity accomplishes the exact same thing!* If you like the idea of having a stable pension instead of a large portfolio, then annuities are one way to accomplish this.

Pros:

You know exactly what your income will be for the duration of the contract. Annuities offer pretty strong protection of your money through Assuris (which we'll explain a little later).

Cons:

You can lose purchasing power if inflation increases. Once you sign the annuity contract, you cannot change your mind – you have given up your assets in exchange for guaranteed income.

A FEW MORE KEY THINGS TO KNOW...

Since the lump sum you spend to purchase an annuity is often invested by the insurance company in fixed income investments (such as bonds), with the low interest rates that exist today annuities will earn less than when interest rates are high – and therefore will pay you less. However as you get older, a large part of the return is based on mortality rates (the fact that some people will be subsidizing your annuity payments as explained in the example earlier). Knowing this, you shouldn't buy an annuity until you are going to need the income. This shouldn't be an "all or nothing" decision. There is nothing wrong with taking a portion of your assets and buying an annuity this year while leaving the rest of your investment alone. Then a few years later you might want to take a little more money and buy another annuity – so you have a few annuity contracts providing you with an income. Let me explain with an example:

Suppose you have managed to save up $500,000 and you have a typical investment portfolio of stocks and bonds. Let's assume at the age of 66, you decided to take $100,000 of your portfolio and buy an annuity. Then at age 69, you take an additional $100,000 and buy another annuity (maybe with a different insurer to avoid putting all your eggs in the same basket). Then when you are 71 there is a financial panic and your portfolio has been reduced, but you still receive your steady annuity income as promised. Then at age 73, the markets have calmed down and your portfolio has recovered, so you buy another $100,000 annuity. Perhaps you decide to keep the remaining $200,000 invested in your portfolio and keep control of that money. You are now receiving three separate income streams from three different annuities – steady income you can rely on that will help reduce your financial worries.

BUT ARE THEY SAFE?

One question you might be thinking is, "If I buy a GIC from a bank or put money in a savings account, I am protected by the Canada Deposit Insurance Corp (CDIC) for up to $100,000. But what about annuities – how safe are they? If the insurance company suddenly goes bankrupt, where does that leave me?"

In Canada there is an organization called Assuris (which was founded in 1990) whose function is to protect Canadian policy holders if their life insurance companies should fail. In addition, *every life insurance company authorized to sell insurance policies in Canada is required by regulators to become a member of Assuris.*

For annuity income, Assuris guarantees that if your insurance company fails you will be entitled to $2,000 per month or 85% of your promised income (whichever is higher). Once again, since the full guarantee tops out at $2,000 per month, if you are buying annuities for greater income, you might wish to spread your investments around to a few different insurers for added safety (the same way some investors have money at different banks for added security).

For a quick look at history, it's important to note that Assuris has been tested a few times since its creation which has allowed it to learn how to deal with insolvencies of life insurance companies. Two examples of how Assuris has done would be the winding up and liquidation of Sovereign Life and Confederation Life in the 1990s.

In 1993, a winding up order was granted against Sovereign Life. The vast majority of the approximately 249,000 policy holders (around 96%) were fully protected by Assuris. Of the 4% of clients who were not fully protected, all of them retained at least 90% of their benefits.

A little over a year after the demise of Sovereign Life was the liquidation of Confederation Life. This company had operations in Canada, the United Kingdom, and the United States. In Canada, there were around 260,000 individual policy holders in addition to around 1.5 million people who were part of group insurance plans.

In spite of the size of this company, there was a full financial recovery for all policy holders.

The point is that although nothing is absolutely certain, the existence of Assuris adds an extra layer of protection if you decide that annuities might be a reasonable option for you to create additional income in retirement.

WHAT TYPES OF ANNUITIES CAN YOU BUY?

There are many different types of annuities in existence and which one you choose depends on what you are trying to accomplish. Let's go over a few of the basic ones here:

1. **Life Annuity**

   This is the most basic plain vanilla annuity. You pay a lump sum and receive a predetermined income for the rest of your life. How much you receive will depend on interest rates (the higher interest rates are, the more money you receive) and also your age (sine the insurance company is giving you money for the rest of your life, the older you are when you buy the annuity, the higher your monthly income will be).

* Note – you can also purchase a life annuity which will guarantee that you (or your family) receive the payments for a certain number of years (for example – guaranteed for 15 years). If you choose this guarantee, your initial monthly payments will be a little lower, but you will be guaranteed to receive payments for a certain amount of time.

2. **Joint and Last Survivor Annuity**

   This is the annuity suitable for couples which guarantees an income for the duration of both you and your spouse's lives. Within this option, you can choose to keep payments at the same level in the event of one spouses death or have them reduced somewhat if one of the spouses die (If you structure it such that the amount decreases upon the death of a spouse, your initial monthly payment will be higher).

3. **Annuity Certain**

   With this annuity, you pay a lump sum and are guaranteed an income for a set number of years (not necessarily as long as you live). For example, you could purchase an annuity which will guarantee payments until you reach the age of 90.

* Note – You can also purchase indexed annuities which increase their payments over time to compensate for inflation. For example, you can choose an annuity which increases payments based on the overall inflation rate or you can have the payments increase by a set percentage each year (ex. payments increase at 2% per year). With these options, you will receive a lower initial monthly cash payment.

As an aside, CPP and OAS are essentially life annuities provided by the government and indexed to inflation.

There a many various twists and unique options you can add to annuity contracts, but I just want to provide a basic overview without getting too bogged down with all the specifics. If you wish to use an annuity in your retirement planning, you will need to contact an insurance company which can provide you with more specific information and show you the various options. Finally, remember this – nothing is "free" so for every option you ask for, you will be giving something up (usually a lower monthly income amount).

Remember: The Taxman *Always* Get Paid...

Just a quick look at taxes with annuities because they are a large consideration...

If you buy an annuity with RRSP money, each payment you received will be taxed like regular income. In effect you are taxed on the money you receive as if you are working (except you don't have to work to earn it and you don't pay other deductions such as CPP, EI, etc).

If you use regular savings to buy an annuity (money not inside your RRSP), things get a little trickier. If you invest a lump sum into an annuity, you will get a certain amount of cash paid to you every year (some of which will be taxed and some of which won't because it is considered a return of your original invested money). Don't worry about the ins and outs, just

remember that part of the money you receive
will not be taxable.

* Note: If you want to receive the same
amount of money (after-tax) every month,
then you should buy a *Prescribed Annuity.*

Let's use a simple example to explain how
the taxes will work:

Suppose you have $100,000 and you buy
a life annuity which pays you $7,000 per
year. We'll assume you choose a prescribed
annuity and your tax bracket is 40%. If
$3,000 is deemed taxable and $4,000 is
deemed non-taxable, this is how it would
look *after-tax:*

Taxable Amount $3,000

Tax Rate   40%

Taxes Payable = $3,000 x 40% = $1,200

Your after-tax cash flow would be:

$7,000 (received) minus $1,200

   (taxes payable) = $5,800 per year

So you would receive $5,800 after tax for the rest of
your life.

5. Guaranteed Lifetime Withdrawal Products

The final retirement tool you might consider is known as guaranteed lifetime withdrawal products. These investment products are relatively new in Canada and offered through major insurance companies. The appealing aspect of these products is that they *offer a guaranteed income for life;* which is similar in some ways to annuities.

There are three major differences between these products and annuities:

(a) you can benefit from growth if the investments increase in value

(b) unlike an annuity, you can get some money back in an emergency

(c) the initial cash return will be lower than with an annuity in most cases

Let me briefly explain this in a little more detail. Since these products generally offer a 5% cash payout, if you invest $100,000 into a guaranteed lifetime withdrawal product, you can guarantee yourself ($100,000 X 5%) = $5,000 per year for the rest of your life *regardless of what happens in the financial world.* This guarantee is the appealing feature for many retirees (just as it is with annuities), but there is also another feature.

When you contribute your $100,000, this money will be invested into a segregated fund (which is similar to a mutual fund which will own stocks and bonds). Every 3 years, if your investments have grown in value, you can reset the amount of cash return you receive to a higher amount (but you will never be reset to a lower amount). Let's use an example to explain this:

Suppose you invest $100,000 into one of these products and you begin receiving $5,000 per year. At the end of three years, the segregated funds you invested in have increased in value by a net 25% (after growth, expenses and adjustments), so the value has increased to $125,000. Here's what your income would now be:

$$\$125,000 \times 5\% = \$6,250$$

Your annual income from this product would now be reset to this higher amount.

Let's look at a reverse scenario. What happens if the stock market crashes and your investment account loses value? For example, the value of your investment drops 25%. In this case, you will not reset to a lower amount – you will continue collecting $5,000 per year in income. Even if the value of your account drops to zero, you are still guaranteed the $5,000 per year in income.

As mentioned, another feature is that in the case of an emergency, you can withdraw some money from these plans. There will be fees associated with this and you will only get the value of the plan (in other words if you want to withdraw money and the investment has lost value you can only withdraw the lower amount). With the fees and risk associated with this option, it is always best to keep emergency cash on hand outside of these investments in a regular savings account or something similar.

Overall, I think you can probably get higher returns with other investments, but many retirees like the peace of mind these products provide (for a portion of their retirement savings).

Pros:

You get a guaranteed income for life with the potential that your income will rise over time (if the investments perform well as shown in the example). In the event of an emergency, you can withdraw your money based on the value of your plan.

Cons:

The fees are quite high. Nothing is free in this world and you are paying for the guaranteed aspect of the plan. In addition, although the income is guaranteed, there is no guaranteed protection against inflation. Even if $5,000 is the amount of money you are earning today, that same $5,000 will probably buy a lot less 10-20 years from now. The initial income generated by annuities will generally be higher than with these plans in most cases, so compare the two options before you invest.

This covers most of the common investment tools you have available to you. You can augment your retirement arsenal by using some of the ideas I offered in my book, "*STOP WORKING TOO: You Still Can!*". I won't go into them again here, but you might consider putting a mortgage inside your RRSP or RRIF to get much higher interest rates than those available through conventional GICs, you may want to take a look at preferred shares, or invest in stocks conservatively to guarantee that you never lose money. These topics are covered in detail in that previous book.

The important point to remember is that for a comfortable retirement, you are looking at creating a good, stable, and reliable income – you're not obsessing about increasing your wealth. For example, when looking at stocks you should be focusing on dividends rather than hoping for a big gain in price. Forget "buy low, sell high!" you're more interested in, "buy reasonable, then sit on your (ass)ets and collect the dividends". Remember:

> *To create a good retirement **outcome**,*
> *you need to create a good retirement*
> ***income**!*

Now that you have a fully stocked financial toolbox available to you and a good idea of your expenses in retirement, you can complete the retirement action workbook section to get a clear idea of your future financial situation. Once that's done, you should be able to construct a worry-free retirement plan for yourself. But what if you don't like using these tools?

What if you don't want to spend the time to do this? What if you wish you simply had a pension? The next chapter will look at how you can join a pension plan that you might not have known is available to you...

A Pension Plan For YOU – Even if Your Employer Doesn't Offer One!

---

*"Companies are doing everything they
can to get rid of pension plans and
they will succeed."*

Ben Stein

Most people buy a house at some point in their lives but a small minority of people actually build their own houses. They plan the design and subcontract all the work until the job is fully completed. In many cases the price is cheaper doing it yourself and you get exactly what you want. A reasonable question might be, "Why doesn't everyone build their own house?".

The answer is that many people don't know the first thing about building a house so the whole process seems daunting. In addition, working with subcontractors can create no end of stress...if they don't show up on time or don't do what they promised. This is why many people buy a new or existing home – the simplicity of going this route. It can be the same with planning your retirement. Joining a pension plan to give you some added income might be a reasonable route for you.

Politicians have been discussing different options to boost retirement pensions because many people will not have sufficient income to fund their retirement. There has been talk of increasing CPP or offering other alternatives to Canadians. The reality is that baby boomers are reaching the point where they are focused on their retirements and with the boomers representing such a large portion of the population, this discussion will only get louder over time. But do you really want to trust your financial future to the chattering political class? Do you want to wait to see what plan they come up with – if anything? Personally, I always prefer to take control of my own destiny rather than trust "the establishment" to provide for me – so here's a simple option for you... There is already a little-known pension that is open to absolutely anyone who is a resident of Canada – called the Saskatchewan Pension Plan.

> *Important Note: You **do not** have to be a resident of Saskatchewan to join this pension – you simply have to be a resident of Canada.*

I think this plan is a reasonable option for many people who are not interested in spending a lot of time reading and researching about investing – so let's take a closer look at it.

A LITTLE BACKGROUND:

The Saskatchewan Pension Plan (SPP) was created through the Saskatchewan Pension Plan Act. Starting over 25 years ago in 1986, the plan has grown over the years and it now boasts over 30,000 plan members.

HOW DOES IT WORK?

The SPP is open to any Canadian resident between the ages of 18-71. You are allowed to contribute up to $2,500 per year into the plan (but there is a little loophole I will mention a little later that can boost your contribution amounts). In order to contribute, you must have contribution room inside your RRSP. This should not be a problem for most people because if you are employed and do not have any company pension plan, you will be able to contribute up to 18% of your employment income into your RRSP.

> *If you join the Saskatchewan Pension Plan, any contribution you make will be tax-deductible (just like an RRSP).*

An Example of How it Works:

Let's look at an example to get a better understanding. Suppose you are in the 30% tax bracket (which occurs at incomes of around $40,000/year). You decide to contribute $200 per month (which would be $2,400 for the year). Here's the result:

Amount You Contribute	$2,400
Less: Tax Deduction ($2,400 X 30%)	–$ 720
Net Amount You Paid	$1,680

From this example, you would contribute $2,400 over the year but then you would get $720 back from the government at tax time for a net contribution amount of $1,680. You would now have a balance of $2,400 invested in your pension plan. This is similar to how a regular RRSP works. The funny thing is that you have probably never noticed this option of joining the SPP – but it shows the deduction right there on your income tax form. Simply go to line 209 of your T1 General (your tax form) and you will see it.

Making contributions is also easy. You can go into your bank or mail in your contribution if you like to do things the old-fashioned way. Or if you don't even want to think about it, you can set up a pre-authorized payment plan through your bank and have the contributions automatically taken out of your account semi-monthly, monthly, semi-annually, or annually.

You can schedule the payments to be taken out on the 1ˢᵗ of the month or the 15th. And finally, I never thought I would see this, but you can make your contribution with your Visa or MasterCard online at ***www.saskpension.com*** (it seems strange that you could contribute to your pension with a credit card and collect points for free groceries or air travel at the same time).

A "LOOPHOLE" FOR YOU TO BOOST YOUR PENSION

The contributions to the SPP are tax-deductible but they impose a $2,500 annual contribution limit. This amount can grow quite substantially for someone starting in their 20s or 30s, but if you are older than this, you might want to be contributing more every year. Well you can transfer up to $10,000 per year into the Saskatchewan Pension Plan from your existing RRSP. If you have a lot of RRSP contribution room, there is nothing stopping you from contributing the regular $2,500 directly to the SPP while at the same time opening up a simple RRSP savings account and then transferring

$10,000 per year from that account into the SPP. (To find out your excess RRSP contribution room, look at the bottom of your Notice of Assessment sent to you from the Canada Revenue Agency every year after tax time).

Here's one way you could make the transfer (there might be a cheaper way to do this, but I do not know the rules and fees of every financial institution in Canada). You could simply open a PC Financial RRSP account (or check other online banks you might be familiar with) and open up one of the regular interest RRSP accounts. Then once the money hits the account, you can transfer most of it to the SPP (you might want to leave a little money in there to keep the account active). You will incur a $50 fee from PC Financial to transfer this money, but then you will be able to fund your pension much more substantially.

* Note: Since you are opening this RRSP savings account in order to transfer money to the SPP, DO NOT OPEN AN RRSP GIC ACCOUNT. A GIC is a guaranteed investment account and you will

probably see a higher interest rate offered – but with this account you are locking in your money, so you will not be able to transfer money into the SPP.

If you only have 10-15 years until retirement, the difference will be huge. If you contribute the limit of $2,500 per year for 10 years, you will only have contributed $25,000 by the time you need your money, but using the transfer "loophole" will allow you to contribute up to 5 times as much.

WHY THIS PLAN MIGHT BE GOOD FOR YOU

There are a number of appealing aspects of this plan. For starters – it's easy. You simply come up with your contribution whenever you want (it's voluntary, so if something comes up, you can skip a contribution – or stop altogether if need be).

The other benefit is that the cost of administering the plan is fairly low (averaging around 1% per year) whereas many typical mutual funds charge 2% or more. Most RRSPs and other investments are offered by private financial companies who are motivated to make a profit. In contrast, the SPP does not exist to make a profit. Once the expenses have been paid the rest of the money is invested into the plan.

You might ask, "Who cares about a measly 1% difference between mutual funds and the SPP?" Let's take a look at the difference.

Suppose you are considering two investment products and each returns 8% per year before expenses. Investment "A" charges a 1% management fee while Investment "B" charges a 2% fee. After expenses, "A" will earn 7% per year while "B" will earn 6% per year. You are planning to invest $10,000 per year for 25 years. Take a look at the difference:

Investment "A" (1% fee):
$10,000 @ 7% for 25 years = $632,490

Investment "B" (2% fee):
$10,000 @ 6% for 25 years = $548,645

The difference works out to around $84,000!

WHAT ABOUT THE PERFORMANCE
OF THE PLAN?

Let's take a look at the track record. The pension plan has been operating for a little over 25
years (since 1986) – a pretty long-term track
record we can look. During this time, they've
managed to earn an average of 8% per year with
a balanced portfolio (a balanced portfolio consists of stocks and bonds and this approach
reduces risk and volatility over time). This is a
pretty darn respectable return over time – but
let's looks closely at the first decade of the new
millennium (a period which included 2 massive
stock market crashes – the blow-up of the hi-
tech sector after 9/11 in 2001-2002 and also
the financial credit crises of 2008-2009). How
did the fund fare during this difficult climate?
* Note: I have listed the results of the SPP from
2000-2010 and compared it to the TSX Com-
posite and the S&P 500. The TSX is a basket of
Canadian stocks and the S&P is a basket of US
Stocks.

Year	SPP	TSX	S&P
2000	8.96%	1.7%	-9.11%
2001	5.87%	-12.2%	-11.98%
2002	2.86%	-12.8%	-22.27%
2003	7.84%	19.3%	28.72%
2004	10.30%	13.9%	10.82%
2005	10.10%	22.9%	4.79%
2006	12.50%	17.4%	15.74%
2007	-0.30%	7.8%	5.46%
2008	-16.20%	-35.5%	-37.22%
2009	12.70%	30.7%	27.11%
2010	9.40%	14.4%	14.32%

What would have happened if you had invested $10,000 into each of the three options at the beginning of the year 2000? Here is how much you would have today (rounded to the nearest dollar):

SPP	$ 18,008
TSX	$ 15,870
S&P	$ 10,330

The SPP has done better than the Canadian and US stock indexes – but this decade has not been good to stocks generally, so this factor gives the SPP an advantage (since it holds both stocks and bonds). However, this is what you want from retirement funds – some growth and some safety. Let's go over these results in a little more detail. As you can see, the SPP tends to offer returns that are much more stable than the Canadian or US stock markets (because it is a balanced fund which includes some bonds). As you can see, during severe stock market downturns, the SPP held up pretty well. In fact the worst result in the funds history was the -16.2% during the height of the financial crisis – but that is pretty good when compared to the massive declines of the Canadian and US stock markets (of over 35% each)! I checked the historical data and the SPP has only had two losing years from it's inception in 1986 all the way to 2010.

I love stocks and the stock market and over time I feel stocks will offer better returns to investors. However, by owning only stocks you are getting on a huge financial roller-coaster where your portfolio value can go up and down quickly. If you prefer less worry and you are closer to retirement, a fund like the SPP makes sense. It all depends on how much risk you are prepared to take...

PUTTING IT ALL TOGETHER – HOW THIS CAN WORK FOR YOU...

If you don't know a lot about investing the "set and forget" aspect of this plan should appeal to you. Let's take a few minutes to put it all together for you.

The first thing you should realize is that there are two phases you deal with in this pension plan (or any other pension for that matter). The first phase is the accumulation phase – where you are contributing to the plan and accumulating assets. With the SPP, you can contribute up until the year you turn 71 (but you can stop contributing earlier than that if you want). You can also start taking out money from the pension anytime between the ages of

55-71 so you have to determine when you want to retire.

In simple terms, here's how it would all fit together. During your remaining working years, you would contribute to the SPP (up to $2,500 per year or up to $12,500 per year with the "transfer loophole") and invest that money into the SPP. Within the SPP there are two basic investment vehicles. They are:

1, The balanced portfolio
2. The short-term fund

The balanced portfolio consists of a variety of stocks and bonds and the purpose of this option is to build wealth. The short-term fund invests in less volatile short-term investments which will mostly preserve your wealth (but won't increase it). Generally the strategy would be to contribute to the balanced portfolio to allow your pension to grow over time. Once you are a few years away from retiring, you would gradually transfer a percentage of your assets from the balanced portfolio into the short-term fund. By doing this, you are protecting your portfolio's value – just in case there are some unforeseen events such as a major stock market crash.

> * Note – The SPP allows up to two transfer per year free of charge – so rather than making a series of smaller transfers, you should plan for a couple of larger transfers per year if you're at that stage.

Once you reach your retirement, you have to decide what you want to do with this money – and this is the second phase of the plan. You can transfer your portfolio into a Registered Retirement Income Fund or convert it into an annuity (which will provide you a regular income stream as we looked at in the last chapter). If you prefer having control over your investments, the RRIF route might be better. Instead if you prefer to have a steady income stream, then the annuity is the best option.

* Note: The SPP allows you to transfer
your money to a RRIF or purchase an
annuity, or *do a combination of the
options – the choice is yours. So you can
buy an annuity with some of the money
and roll the rest into your RRIF.*

What is a RRIF? A RRIF is similar to an
RRSP in the sense that you can hold assets that
grow tax-free until you withdraw them. The
main difference is if you have a RRIF, you are
obligated to take a percentage of your portfolio
out every year (as mandated by the government).

Pros:

This pension plan is simple – you contribute
what you like (up to the mandated maxi-
mums) and the fund is run automatically for
you. The fees are reasonable and all other
money is used for the benefit of plan holders. Some options are available to you on
how to allocate your money once you retire.
Contributions are tax-deductible (the same
as with RRSPs).

Cons:

You have little control over your portfolio (if you are a sophisticated investor and prefer to invest for yourself) . There are fewer annuity options than are available from insurance companies.

Now let's move on and look at a quick retirement checklist you can use.

YOUR BASIC
RETIREMENT CHECKLIST

———

*"I am prepared for the worst, but hope
for the best."*
Benjamin Disraeli

It's very difficult to create an exact plan for you
to retire because your situation will be as
unique to you as your finger print – there are
simply too many factors to consider to even
attempt to offer a "one size fits all" template.
However, here is a basic checklist you should
follow to cover most of the bases.

1. Be totally debt-free and mortgage-free

2. Have a reliable income that covers basic living expenses

3. Have additional income which covers some FUN

4. Have some cash or short term deposits in case of emergencies

5. Have some stocks to protect against inflation

6. Have some money left over to give away to charities or family members

If you've covered all these bases and have all of the above checked off, chances are you're all set. Let's take a quick look at them a little more closely...

1. Be totally debt-free and mortgage-free

Once you own everything debt-free, life is less stressful and worrisome. If interest rates jump or if the financial world seems to suddenly start to fall apart, YOU DON'T CARE because you don't owe anything to anybody. This was a crucial step I took when I wanted to leave the rat race and it has allowed me to never miss a good night's sleep regardless of what's happening in the world. Do yourself a favour and get out of debt – then enjoy the reassurance of not owing money to anyone.

2. Have a reliable income that covers basic living expenses

If you want to retire, you must have some form of regular income that meets basic living expenses. The Canada Pension Plan and Old Age Security should get you a large part of the way there (although these plans will by no means provide you with a luxurious lifestyle). If you have a pension from your employer, you should be comfortable. If not, you might consider joining the Saskatchewan Pension Plan and/or getting an annuity or a guaranteed income product to take the guesswork out of your future income.

3. Have additional income for FUN

What's the point of retiring and then having to watch how every penny is spent? You need some additional income for fun things like vacations, hobbies, and day-to-day pleasures. Once again, if you have a pension from work, this might cover these expenses. If not, some form of income from annuities or guaranteed income products is a reasonable option. You could also earn interest on investments such as GICs or bonds. And of course, you might hold some blue chip dividend-paying stocks which are in the habit of increasing their dividends regularly. If you are very motivated and don't mind the potential headaches (most people don't want the hassle), you could also own investment real estate and collect rent.

4. Have some cash on hand for emergencies

This is money in savings accounts with the bank or in money market funds. Remember to make sure your money is CDIC insured (all major banks are). This money should be able to be withdrawn very quickly just in case of emergencies.

5. Have some stocks (or real estate) to protect against inflation

Unless you have an indexed pension from your employer, it might be a good idea to own some stocks (or real estate) to protect you from inflation. As prices rise, the prices of the products or services of the companies whose stocks you own should also rise, so the companies make more money and increase their dividends over time – allowing you to keep pace with inflation. But does this really work?

You might have read that since the 1930s, the dollar has lost around 97% of its value (meaning prices of standard items should now be around 33 times as expensive – on average). As a quick example, have you ever seen those old "Drink Coca-Cola" signs that were made 60-plus years ago? At the bottom corner of the signs you always see the price "5 cents". Using the simple idea

that its price should be around 33 times as expensive today, a Coke from a vending machine should cost you around:
(5 cents X 33) = $1.65.

Whenever I pass a vending machine, I have noticed that a Coke usually costs between $1.50 – $2.00. In general prices have risen to match inflation. Since the prices have risen, investors have earned more profits and dividends, which has protected them from inflation.

6. Have some money left over to give to charities or family members

There are countless ways of giving money to charity using life insurance and annuities with a guaranteed payout. I am not an estate planning expert by any stretch, but if leaving money to charity is something that is important to you, speaking to the appropriate professional might provide you with the most tax-efficient way, but these strategies are not really the aim of this book.

If you have set yourself up so that you are financially secure and you are no longer worried about your finances, you are then free to give money or investments to family members. Why leave money to family members after you're gone when you can instead enjoy the benefit of seeing the happiness your gift might bring earlier? We'll get into giving money to family members (and an effective way to do it) in a little more detail in the last chapter, but first I'd like to touch on one final subject you might want to think about.

How Much Would You Pay for a Good Night's Sleep?

"Insurance: An ingenious game of chance where the player is permitted to enjoy the conviction that he is beating the man who keeps the table."
Ambrose Bierce

Our family has been down to Orlando, Florida a few times. Since we have 7 people in the family, it makes a lot more sense to drive rather than fly, so we usually take a couple of days to get to our destination. Usually by the evening of the first night we look for a reasonable place to sleep for the night – there are many of them.

The cost is usually around $75 US, but it's worth it for everyone to get a good night's sleep. Of course, if a traveller were on an extremely tight budget they could always park at the side of a gas station or Wal-Mart. However, they would get a terrible sleep and it might not be safe. So that is the price we pay for a good night's sleep. So the question is...How much would you pay to get a good night's sleep *every night* during your retirement? By this I mean that you would not have to worry about the unexpected.

The previous chapters have looked at various investment tools that can help fund your retirement but this chapter is going to look at providing you with peace of mind. This chapter will look at possible insurance options you might want to consider.

Let me say this right off the bat – I am NOT a huge fan of insurances *in most cases.* Insurance is generally a mathematical equation and a lot of insurance that is sold is complete garbage. As a general rule, the *sellers* of insurance make out much better than the *buyers* of insurance. This is why you can see huge insurance companies make nice profits over time.

Sales pitches are created to get you to buy insurance from many different sources. For example, if you've ever bought any electronic item, chances are that you were offered an extended warranty. In many cases, the company has a good idea of how long the product should last and then sells you this insurance at a price where on average, they can make a profit. In *most* cases this insurance will not be worth the money for you. I generally refuse it unless it is an item my 5 kids will be handling often – in which case I buy it. For example, I opted for the extra warranty when I bought my cordless phone set and I've used it three times – so it was definitely worth the cost. But I passed when we bought our flat screen TV (which sits up fairly high – out of reach of the kids).

In most cases, I opt out of insurance. For example, I have never bought life insurance in my life. Since a large portion of our family income is passive income, if I were to die my family would not face financial hardship – so why would I buy life insurance? I also have never purchased collision insurance on my vehicle (which pays for repairing your own vehi-

cle if you are "at-fault" in an accident). I understand that I might have an accident and be
forced to pay to repair my vehicle, but that
would not ruin me financially, so I can bear this
risk to save the premiums. I also keep a high
deductible on my house insurance for the same
reason. By taking these steps, you can lower
your premiums. I save hundreds of dollars every
year and it would not be catastrophic if I needed
to cover any of these potential losses myself. As
a general rule:

> *Insurance companies are NOT charities –*
> *they are in business to make money. In*
> *most cases, insurance is a bad deal for*
> *you – so DON'T waste your money buy-*
> *ing insurance that you don't really need!*

Having said all that, you should buy insurance against possible catastrophic losses. For
example, since my house is mortgage-free, I am
not obligated to buy fire insurance but I do. It's
the same with auto insurance – I buy much
more liability insurance than the legally mandated minimum amount because I don't want
to face the possibility (however remote) of facing

financial catastrophe. This is my thinking on this:

> *Insurance SHOULD be purchased for situations where you could be financially devastated and lose your entire life savings in the event of a mishap.*

Using this thinking, if I had a large mortgage and did not have investments which generated passive income and I was the sole income earner for my family, I would definitely buy life insurance. If I could not afford a new vehicle if I were to get into an accident, I would buy collision insurance. I would buy insurance that protected me against these potentially terrible financial outcomes.

How does this relate to your retirement? If you are at the stage where you're planning for your retirement, life insurance is probably not necessary for you because your children are probably grown up and on their own.

However, critical illness is one type of insurance (which offers a cash payout to help you if you get an unforeseen illness), which might suitable for you. This insurance can be useful to make sure a major illness does not derail your retirement plans. As you get older this insurance becomes very expensive because the risk of you needing it increases. You would have to get a quote to see if it is affordable at your stage in life and then make your decision.

There is another uncommonly used but potentially useful insurance product that you may consider. It is called long-term care insurance. This type of insurance offers protection in the event that you require long-term care. It is paid if you cannot perform at least a couple of the major activities of daily living (ADLs) which include dressing, bathing, eating, toileting, transferring (getting in and out of bed), and walking. As you get older your chances of possibly needing long-term care increases, so a quick look at potential costs versus possible protection might be something you want to think about. If you require long-term care at some point, it can be very costly. This insurance would help ensure that you have the financial resources to maintain your dignity in the event that you require care. Once again, you would have to compare the costs with the potential protection.

The main point is that as you get older, certain types of insurance may no longer be required while others might be. You want to make sure that unforeseen issues don't affect your lifestyle. Obviously this protection costs money, so you would have to look at your own situation before making a decision. Now let's take a look at an effective way you might give money to family members.

GIVING GIFTS – DO IT RIGHT!

"The empires of the future are the empires of the mind."
Winston Churchill

HELPING YOUR CHILDREN OR GRANDCHILDREN

One of the best pieces of financial advice I ever read mentioned that people should treat their finances like the oxygen masks on airplanes. On every flight I have ever taken, right before the plane takes off; the flight crew spend a few minutes explaining all the safety procedures and equipment on the plane. The interesting thing for any parents who have ever flown with a child is the explanation about how to use the oxygen masks (required if cabin pressure drops). The instinct of most parents is to protect their children at all costs. Most parents would think nothing of diving into shark invested waters to rescue their child from danger – regardless of the consequences they themselves might face. At the beginning of every flight, the flight crew reminds parents that if oxygen masks are needed, the best course of action is to go against your instincts and put your own mask on first before helping your child with their mask. This might seem odd, but if you struggle with your child's mask first and then pass out due to lack of oxygen because you didn't get your own mask on – both you and your child are in trouble!

It's the same with finances. Some people worry about funding their children's education *even when they haven't adequately planned for their own financial futures*. In my opinion, you should make sure that your own situation is taken care of before looking after your kids. In a perfect world you would like to give your loved ones everything they want or need, but reality is that is not always possible. However, once your own financial house is in order, you might want to look at helping family members. Funding education is one thing many people think of. Another option some people might consider is leaving something more for their children or grandchildren.

But how do you do this effectively? Suitable investments for one age group are often unsuitable for other age groups. As life changes, investments should also change. As an example of how things change, let's take a quick look at how a modern holiday has evolved over time...

During the 1800s, Irish immigrants brought an October 31 celebration to the United States. At that time, it was customary to make "soul cakes" and offer them to visitors in return for promises of prayers for dead relatives. This custom morphed over time so that by the time WWII was over, the modern day practised of "trick-or-treating" gained widespread acceptance. Children went door to door to "beg" for treats – which often consisted of candied apples, popcorn balls, and various nuts. Some people simply gave apples and a few people offered packaged candies and chocolate. Over time, as savvy chocolate and candy companies spotted an incredible opportunity – manufactured treats made specifically for the occasion became the norm.

But what on earth does this have to do with investing? It shows how perspectives change over time. For example, I remember going trick or treating as a kid and getting mostly candies and the occasional chocolate bar. But I also remember getting an apple from time to time – usually from an elderly person who remembered getting apples when they were children. I would always politely say "thank you", but in reality I did not really want to get apples. I could not understand why people gave apples. But a quick look at the history of Halloween shows you why this was common for some older people.

It's the same with investing. I have tried to offer some low-risk ideas for you to secure your own retirement, but the kind of investment you choose for yourself might be entirely different than the types of investments you might want to leave your loved ones. For example, I know that there are a lot of older people that have given their grandkids Canada Savings Bonds over the years – and it's a great thought (giving something of lasting value rather than a trinket that ends up in the garbage a month or two after Christmas). These "investments" might seem great to these older people, but when you are giving an investment to someone who is much younger, they will finish *miles ahead* financially if you instead give them small pieces of good quality companies. Even though YOU might be at the stage where you wouldn't want to risk too much money in the stock market, for younger people, stocks are overwhelmingly the best investment option in most cases.

I won't get into it in great detail here because I've already written about it extensively in *The Lazy Investor: Start with $50 and NO Investment Knowledge* – but the absolute best financial legacy you can leave your children or grand-children would be to buy a few shares in a couple of great dividend-paying companies and enrol them in DRIPs (dividend reinvestment plans). Conservative investments are great for older investors, but for young investors, there is nothing like the stock market (or more specif-ically good quality dividend stocks) to create wealth!

ONE MORE IMPORTANT POINT ON TAXES...

Understand that I am not a taxation or legal expert so seek out the appropriate expert to learn all the ins and outs of this, but if you gradually buy shares for family members over time, any dividend income generated will create a tax liability for you. The way to avoid this is to use the recipient's income to buy shares – let me explain with a simple example...

Suppose you would like to buy some shares for your grandchildren but don't want the tax liability. The easiest way to avoid tax issues is for you to speak to their parents and find out if they receive the Child Tax Benefit for the child. If they do, get them to make a separate bank account for the Child Tax Benefit money for each child and use that money to buy the shares. Then simply give the parents the equivalent amount of money as a gift. This way you avoid any unwanted tax consequences.

A SMALL GIFT NOW CAN REALLY GROW...

Even a gift of $50 or $100 can grow immensely over time using DRIPs. As a real-life example of the power of investing in great companies (and using the "Lazy Investor" strategy of enrolling in DRIPs), take a second to Google the name "Grace Groner". This lady lived a low-profile life and worked as a secretary. Her life was fairly normal in every way except one...early in her life she bought 3 shares of the company she worked for (Abbott Labs) and enrolled in a DRIP. This initial $180 investment grew to over $7 million dollars! Canada Savings Bonds will NEVER do that!

My point is that if you want to leave some sort of financial legacy to your family – look at potential investments through their eyes – not yours.

Now that you have learned about YOUR investment options, it's time for YOU to take action!

Part III

—

ACTION!

RETIREMENT ACTION WORKBOOK

—

WORKBOOK SECTION:

*"It pays to plan ahead. It wasn't rain-
ing when Noah built the Ark."*

\- Unknown

Many books have been written which say that
you need a certain percentage of your working
income in retirement...for example, 70% of your
working income. I think this type of planning

does not take into account personal circumstances. This sort of approach to planning is like a doctor having a standard list of medications people over a certain age require and prescribing them to you without actually doing a medical exam – how silly would that seem? This workbook section will create a starting point for you.

These are calculations that can be challenging for some people. If this describes you, this is an area where you might want to get some advice from a financial advisor. This is a task where a good advisor really earns their keep and most competent advisors will be able to estimate your future income using their own software. If you prefer to figure this out for yourself, here is the information you need...

YOUR FINANCIAL SNAPSHOT...
IN THE FUTURE!

This step involves some guesswork – but since you already calculated your current expenses earlier, you should be able to get a pretty accurate picture of what your future expenses will look like once you retire.

> * Note: To keep things simple, we will not worry about price increases (inflation) in your calculations – just think of what sort of expenses you will have and we'll calculate them *based on what they cost today*. We will make the necessary adjustments to your calculations a little later.

In order to get as accurate a picture as you can, you need to have an idea of what you want. If you are married, sit down with your spouse and make sure what your life goals are. For example, do you want to downsize your current house or stay put? Do you want to buy a cottage or recreational property? Is travel in your plans? Any new activities you want to do? These questions are crucial if you want to get an accurate idea of what your future expenses will be. In addition, make revisions based on real-life realities – NOT blind hopes. For example, if you are making mortgage payments right now but plan to be mortgage-free when you retire, great – but make sure you are indeed on track to become mortgage-free. If you plan to retire in 5 years but have 12 years left on your mortgage amortization, you can't assume you will not be making mortgage payments when you retire unless you have implemented an actual plan to pay off your mortgage early *and you are following that plan.* You have to be honest with yourself. Also take into account all the changes that will happen between now and when you retire. If you have two university kids living at home right now but they will be on their own by the time you retire, that will greatly reduce your grocery bill along with some other expenses (especially if you are paying part or all of their tuition).

Once you have all the information, complete the following chart for your expected retirement expenses (using today's prices):

Expenses when

you retire   **Monthly Cost**

HOUSING

Mortgage/Rent   _____

Line of Credit   _____

Property Taxes   _____

Insurance   _____

Maintenance   _____

Electricity   _____

Gas/Heating   _____

Water   _____

Home Phone   _____

Cell Phone   _____

Cable/Satellite   _____

Internet   _____

Other housing expenses   _____

Total housing expenses   _____ ➔ _____

TRANSPORTATION

Car #1 Loan/Lease   _____

Car #2 Loan/Lease   _____

Other Cars Loan/Lease   _____

Gas (all cars)   _____

Insurances (all cars)   _____

Maintenance (all cars)   _____

Parking costs   _____

Public Transportation   _____

Total transportation
  expenses   _____ ➔ _____

FOOD

Groceries   _____

Dining Out   _____

Quick Food
  (Coffee, Muffins, etc)   _____

Total Food Costs   _____ ➔ _____

OTHER EXPENSES

Child Care _____

School Tuition _____

Entertainment _____

Hair/Beauty Services _____

Club Memberships _____

Clothing _____

Gifts _____

Medical Costs

   (prescriptions, etc) _____

Vacations _____

Other Insurance

(Life, Pet, etc) _____

Pet care costs _____

Suscriptions

   (magazines, etc.) _____

Debt Payments

   (credit cards, etc) _____

Other (anything not listed) _____

_____

_____

_____

Total Other Expenses _____ ➔ _____

TOTAL EXPENSES IN RETIREMENT _____

The next step in this process is calculating your expected passive pension income. This will take into account your work-related pension (if you have any), Canada Pension Plan (CPP), Old Age Security (OAS), Guaranteed Income Supplement and any other pension income you expect to receive.

If you have a work-related defined benefit pension plan (a pension that promises you a certain income after you retire), contact your employer's human resources office to get a better idea of how much you can expect to earn in pension income once you retire. We already looked at the various government pensions earlier, so you can use the information in that chapter to figure out how much income from these sources you can expect.

> * IMPORTANT NOTE: If you have an employee pension plan, you still can't be certain you will get all the pension income you are expecting. If your employer faces financial difficulties and goes bankrupt, your pension income might be reduced. As an example of what can happen, look at former Nortel

employees whose pensions were affected after Nortel went bankrupt. The more financially stable your employer is, the more certain you can be that your future pension benefits will be paid in full. Currently, many pension plans are underfunded meaning pension recipients may be forced to accept reduced benefits in the future. If you face this potential problem, it might make sense for you to save and invest more money on your own – or join another pension plan such as the Saskatchewan Pension Plan.

Once you have an idea of what your income sources will be, plug them into the chart below *using today's dollar amounts.* In addition, make sure to use *after-tax amounts.* Remember that CPP and OAS mostly automatically adjusts to inflation. Work-related defined pensions are usually based on a percentage of your best five years which also automatically accounts for inflation (because between now and when you retire your salary will probably increase with inflation). If you have a defined contribution pension plan, leave it out of this calculation for now – we will include this amount later. Only include a defined benefit pension plan benefits. (I've defined these two types of plans so you know what kind of pension plan you have, if any):

Defined Contribution Plan – a retirement plan where a certain amount or percentage of money is set aside each year for you. The amount contributed is fixed, but you don't know how much the plan will eventually pay. The value of the pension depends on how well the investments do over time. In a nutshell, these types of plans are kind of similar to an RRSP – except that the employer helps contribute to the plan.

Defined Benefit Plan – a pension plan where the employee receives a promised pension based on a formula such as salary history and duration of employment. These are the traditional types of pensions that most people are familiar with – but they are becoming less common over time.

Expected Pension Income	Monthly Amount
Defined Benefit Pension	_____
Spouse's Defined Pension	_____
CPP (combined spousal)	_____
OAS (combined spousal)	_____
GIS (combined spousal)	_____
Other Income	_____
Other Income	_____
TOTAL PENSION INCOME	_____

If you have a defined pension from work, consider yourself lucky – most workers don't! The absolute "holy grail" of the pension world would be those generous defined benefit pensions based on a percentage of your best 5 years (indexed to inflation) which are provided to many public service workers. In many cases, if you can expect to receive one of these, you will not have to worry about saving much for retirement as this income could very well cover all your living expenses. However, the reality is that many workers will not have any work-related pension. If that includes you, you will have to plan for your retirement.

Now let's take a look at your other income sources such as defined contribution pensions, rental income, dividends, and interest that you can rely on. These investments can be in your (and/or your spouses) RRSP, TFSA, or simply in regular investment accounts.

At this stage we are only looking at investments *you own right now*! We are not accounting for future savings or investments you might make *unless* you are currently contributing a set amount regularly and you are fairly certain these contributions will continue. We want to be conservative and avoid *hoping* for extra money to *appear* when you need it. If you are making regular contributions, you will have to calculate your expected portfolio income from these savings when you retire. You cannot get a precise answer for this, but you have to make a reasonable best guess and then revisit the numbers every year or so. Calculating your income in retirement from these savings is a two-step process. You have to:

1. Figure out how much these savings will grow to, and then,

2. Calculate your expected income from these savings

The first step for you is to assume a portfolio growth rate and use that rate to calculate the expected value of your investment when you plan on retiring. For example, if you are calculating your expected future value of your RRSP and you have invested around half of your money in stocks (or equity mutual funds) with the other half invested in bonds or GICs, you might assume it rises in value at 5% per year. If you have all stocks, you could assume it will rise at 7-8% per year. If you had all fixed income investments such as bonds or GICs, you should assume around 2-3% per year (since interest rates are quite low as of this writing).

If you are good with spreadsheets, you can do these calculations in seconds. If you're not good at spreadsheets, you can do the calculations on paper (which is not too difficult). Here's how to do the calculation to find out how much your portfolio should grow to in value if you are making regular contributions:

> * IMPORTANT: The growth will vary
> from year to year – especially if you own
> stocks or equity mutual funds (mutual
> funds that own stocks), but we are cal-
> culating an expected *average return::*

Amount you have right now in investments: _____

Add: Your annual contribution   +_____

Equals (How much you will have this year) =_____

Multiply by your expected rate of
    growth (ex. 5%)   x 1.05_____

Equals (Your expected
    balance after year 1)   =_____

You would have to repeat this process for every year until your retire (ex. If you are retiring in 20 years, you would do this same calculation 20 times). It sounds difficult, but you can do it in a couple of minutes with a normal calculator.

Let me use an example so that it is totally clear. Suppose you have an investment account which has $100,000 now and you are contributing an extra $20,000 every year (let's assume you earn 5% after inflation every year). How much would you estimate to have in 5 years? Here's what you should have after year one:

($100,000 now + $20,000 contribution) X 1.05

(5% growth) = **$126,000** (after year 1)

This is the amount you estimate to have after year 1, so this would be the amount you begin with in year 2 before adding your regular $20,000 contribution– so it would look like this:

(**$126,000** + $20,000) x 1.05 = **$153,300** (after year 2)

This new amount is then used for year 3:

(**$153,300** + $20,000) x 1.05 = $181,965 (year 3)

($181,965 + $20,000) x 1.05 = $212,063 (year 4)

($212,063 + $20,000) x 1.05 = $243,666 (year 5)

If you wanted to estimate how much you would have in 20 years, you simply have to do the same calculation 20 times.

> *Once again, if you have a large stock component in your portfolio, the year to year values will vary from your estimates. Some years might actually be negative growth while others might be positive. Over a longer time period, your estimated and actual portfolio value growth should be somewhat similar. As you get closer to retirement, the stock component of your portfolio should get smaller to reduce risk.*

You need to do this type of calculation for all investment accounts. This would include: defined contribution pension plans, RRSP accounts, TFSAs, and any other investment account you might have.

Once you have an estimate for the future value of your accounts, you need to estimate how much income it will generate. This is step 2 in the process. A simple way estimate this would be to calculate how much income (interest and dividends) your investments earn now and use that same rate to calculate your future income. Let's use an example to explain:

If you own $100,000 in investments today and you earn $4,000 per year in income from these investments, your rate of return would be:

$4000 divided by $100,000 = 0.04 or 4%

This is the income rate you would use to calculate your future portfolio income (4%). Therefore, using the example we used earlier (where your $100,000 grew to $243,666 with the additional $20,000 contributions every year for 5 years), your expected income in 5 years from our original example would be:

$243,666 (portfolio value) X 0.04
(rate of return of 4%) = $9,747/year

The next step would be to calculate your estimated tax on this income to arrive at your *after tax* income.

For example, if you are in the 30% tax
bracket, your *after-tax* income will be:

$9,747 (portfolio income) minus 30% (taxes)
= $6,823 /year

The final step in the process is to factor in
inflation. Remember with all other calculations
you made, you calculated the amounts in
today's dollars. You have to make the proper
adjustments to make sure your investment
income is also calculated in today's dollars.

The chart on the next page shows you the
number of years down the left-hand column
and the inflation rate across the top.

Year	2%/year	3%/year	4%/year	5%/year
1	1.020	1.030	1.040	1.050
2	1.040	1.061	1.082	1.103
3	1.061	1.093	1.125	1.158
4	1.082	1.126	1.170	1.216
5	1.104	1.159	1.217	1.277
6	1.126	1.194	1.265	1.341
7	1.149	1.230	1.316	1.408
8	1.172	1.267	1.369	1.478
9	1.195	1.305	1.423	1.552
10	1.219	1.344	1.480	1.629
11	1.243	1.384	1.539	1.710
12	1.267	1.426	1.601	1.796
13	1.292	1.469	1.665	1.886
14	1.318	1.513	1.731	1.980
15	1.346	1.558	1.801	2.079
16	1.373	1.605	1.873	2.183
17	1.400	1.653	1.948	2.292
18	1.428	1.703	2.026	2.407
19	1.457	1.754	2.107	2.527
20	1.486	1.806	2.191	2.653
25	1.641	2.094	2.666	3.386

Now that you have this chart, you can figure out how much your future income will be worth in *today's dollars*. Therefore from our earlier example, if you will be earning $6,823 per year in 5 years and we average 3% inflation, here's what you'd do. Go down the left-hand column until you get to 5 (5 years) then go across the top until you see 3% (the inflation rate). The number that corresponds to this is 1.159. This is your inflation factor which you can use to calculate your future income in today's dollars. Here it is:

$6,823 (future income) divided by 1.159 = $5,586

* This amount ($5,886) is your income in today's dollars (accounting for inflation). This is the amount you would enter in the chart below. You would do this same type of calculation for all your accounts (ex. RRSPs, TFSAs, Defined Contribution Plans,)

Investment Income	Monthly Amount
Defined Contribution Pension	_____
Spouses Defined Contribution Pension	_____
Rental Income (Net)	_____
RRSP Acct. (Dividends/Interest)	_____
Spouses RRSP Acct. (Dividends/Interest)	_____
TFSA Acct. (Dividends/Interest)	_____
Spouses TFSA Acct. (Dividends/Interest)	_____
Non-registered Acct. (Dividends/Interest)	_____
Other passive income	_____
TOTAL INVESTMENT INCOME	_____

* Note: DON'T make any adjustments for inflation for rental income. Simply write in how much rental income you receive today – because this number will approximately adjust for inflation automatically over time (as rents rise over time).

Finally, add your pension income (work pension, CPP, OAS, etc) which you entered earlier to your total investment income to figure out your total expected retirement income.

TOTAL PENSION INCOME　　　　　_____

TOTAL INVESTMENT INCOME　　　_____

TOTAL EXPECTED

RETIREMENT INCOME　　　　　　_____

Now you have a rough idea of how much your income and expenses will be in retirement (adjusted to be in today's dollars). Plug these numbers into the appropriate spaces in the Appendix at the back of this book so you can have a quick one-page snapshot to look at.

If your estimated future income is higher than your estimated expenses, you're on the right track. Recheck everything once a year to make sure you stay on target. If your expected expenses are higher than your estimated income, you now know how much extra income you will need to generate in order to eliminate this gap. Light has been shed on the darkness and the unknown has been eliminated. You can use the information in this book to either lower your future spending or increase your future income to meet your retirement goals. The financial tools discussed will give you an idea of how you might be able to boost your expected income.

The lights have been turned on and the camera has taken a snapshot – now it's time for action!

APPENDIX
YOUR FINANCES
–A QUICK SNAPSHOT

"Too many people spend money they haven't earned, to buy things they don't want, to impress people they don't like

Will Smith

CURRENT MONTHLY INCOME AND EXPENSE

1) Total Current Income   _____

2) Total Current Expenses   _____

Surplus or Deficit (1 minus 2)   _____

RETIRED MONTHLY INCOME AND EXPENSES

1) Estimated Retirement Income   _____

2) Estimated Retirement Expenses   _____

Surplus or Deficit (1 minus 2)   _____

Looking for a Speaker for Your Next Event?

Are you looking for a dynamic speaker who is the exact opposite of the stereotypical dry financial speaker? Do you want someone who combines humour and personal stories that capture the attention of your audience?

Derek Foster offers a down-to-earth approach in explaining simple investing concepts that allowed him to become a millionaire and leave the rat race by the time he was 34! He has also written numerous National Bestselling investment books explaining his approach.

He is a highly sought after speaker and has captured the attention of various audiences. TV experiences include interviews on Breakfast Television, CBC "The Hour", ROBTV, and CTV Newsnet along with many others. Derek has also given live presentations across Canada in front of many diverse audiences.

To bring financial speaker Derek Foster to your next event, contact us:

Foster Underhill Financial Press

900 Greenbank Rd, Suite 508, Ottawa, ON K2J 4P6

Telephone: **(613) 823-2143**

Toll-free: **1-888-686-7867**

www.stopworking.ca

FREE E-LETTER
FOR YOU...

Thousands of readers have signed up for my free newsletter which offers investment updates on what is happening in the investing world. If you would like to get a quick update e-mailed to you once a month, here's what you need to do:

Here's how to join (it takes 30 seconds):

Go to: **www.stopworking.ca**

Click on: "Free Newsletter"
                (left side of the page)

Scroll down to the bottom of the page

Click on: The "Click Here" box

Enter your email address, click send, and you're done!

* This service is free and I do not sell or give your email address to any third parties. This is simply a way for me to stay connected with you and keep you updated on investment events as they happen.

RECOMMENDED READING (AND OTHER RESOURCES)

---

*"The man who does not read good
books has no advantage over
the man who can't read."*
Mark Twain

Stop Working Too: You Still Can! (conservative
investment ideas)
Derek Foster

The Idiot Millionaire: You Can Become Wealthy
(a strategy for stock investing)
Derek Foster

The Lazy Investor: Start With $50 and No Investment Knowledge (investing for beginners)
Derek Foster

Stop Working: Here's How You Can! (early retirement strategies)
Derek Foster

Pensionize Your Nest Egg (retirement investing)
Moshe Milevsky and Alexandra Macqueen

The Pension Puzzle (retirement planning)
Bruce Cohen & Brian Fitzgerald

Your Retirement Income Blueprint (retirement income planning)
Daryl Diamond

Canadian MoneySaver Magazine (investment/retirement planning magazine)

The Joy of Not Working (fulfillment in retirement)
Ernie Zelinski

* Note: If you are a baby boomer, you may wish to look at some of the benefits available by joining CARP. This organization offers various discounts and specials for members and the cost seems reasonable. You might also wish to look at Zoomer magazine.